JOHNNY
HAYNES
(Fulham)

YOU ARE THE REF

50 YEARS OF PAUL TREVILLION'S CULT CLASSIC COMIC STRIP

'Fans and professionals should realise how difficult a job the referee has, and ask themselves, "Would I like to change places with him?" I think the answer would be "no", so let's give referees the help and respect they deserve. Yes, they may exasperate and anger us at times, but we simply can't do without them.'

Sir Alex Ferguson CBE, Manchester United

YOU ARE THE REF

50 YEARS OF PAUL TREVILLION'S CULT CLASSIC COMIC STRIP

Edited by David Hills and Giles Richards

TheObserver

First published in 2006 by Observer Books
Observer Books is an imprint of Guardian Newspapers Limited

All illustrations © Paul Trevillion

Collection © The Observer 2006

Layouts and fonts pp 53-55, 58, 59, 61, 64-67, 70-90, 92-95 © Shoot Monthly/IPC+ Syndication

Text, pp 53-55, 58, 59, 61, 66, 67, 70-81 © Stanley Lover
Text, pp 82-89 © Clive Thomas
Text, 90-95, 98-127 © Keith Hackett

A CIP record for this book is available from the British Library upon request

ISBN: 0 85265 069 8
ISBN 13: 978 0 85265 069 1

Cover Design: Two Associates
Interior Page Design: Jane Daniel
Sub-editor: Philip Cornwall
Reproduction: Oliver Spratley

With thanks to Mark Towers of www.royoftherovers.com

Distributed by A&C Black Publishers Ltd

Printed in Great Britain by Cambridge University Press

10 9 8 7 6 5 4 3 2 1

CONTENTS

THE STRIP

DURING A LEAGUE GAME, A PLAYER MANAGES TO CATCH THE BALL IN HIS TURBAN AND RUN 20 YARDS INTO THE GOALMOUTH. WITH 20,000 PEOPLE WATCHING – DO YOU AWARD A GOAL?

You Are The Ref, drawn by sports artist Paul Trevillion and written by top referees, has been entertaining football fans for generations, ever since its newspaper debut in 1957. Featuring a series of awkward refereeing dilemmas, it puts you at the heart of the action, demanding you react instantly, and accurately, to the tricky – sometimes bizarre – situations you face. How well do you know the laws of the game?

The idea for the strip dates back to 1952 when Paul, aged 18, sent a general sports quiz to Spurs magazine *The Lilywhite* (below). Readers loved it, particularly the one question about a tricky refereeing decision. By 1954 the quiz of 10 questions had more than half on referees.

It set Paul thinking – and, three years later, after a struggle to convince the national press that the idea would work, the Ref brand was born, commissioned by *The People* under its first name 'Hey Ref'. But it wasn't until the 1958 FA Cup final, when Bolton's Nat Lofthouse bundled the ball, still held by Manchester United keeper Harry Gregg, into the back of the net for his side's second goal, that it became a regular feature. By the late 50s and early 60s, with Paul also drawing comic art realism stories for Roy of the Rovers, the feature appeared in a new, larger format in the Roy annuals, under the title 'If You Were The Ref'.

'I'd always been into refereeing,' says Paul. 'When I was a goalkeeper at school I kept having goal-hangers scoring offside goals against me. So I spent a whole summer learning how to do a shrill whistle through my teeth. The next season, every time a striker broke through, I blew, he stopped and I picked up the ball. It worked a treat. After a while my science master, Mr Bellingham, worked out what I was doing and told me to stop – but I don't

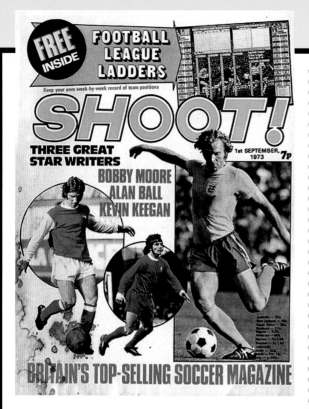

FREE INSIDE

FOOTBALL LEAGUE LADDERS

Keep your own week-by-week record of team positions

SHOOT!

1st SEPTEMBER, 1973 7p

THREE GREAT STAR WRITERS

BOBBY MOORE
ALAN BALL
KEVIN KEEGAN

BRITAIN'S TOP-SELLING SOCCER MAGAZINE

think he was convinced I would, so he bought me a book on the art of refereeing. I never looked back.'

In 1969, the strip moved to the newly launched *Shoot!* magazine (above) and took on referee Stan Lover, head of the London referees' association, to provide the answers. Over the next two decades, working with Stan, Clive 'The Book' Thomas and finally Keith Hackett, the strip became a cult hit.

'The inspiration for it was everywhere,' says Paul. 'I have this photo of Jimmy Greaves about to score against Benfica in the 1962 European Cup – he's onside, but you can see the linesman's flag in the background. It killed me then, and it kills me now.'

But then, after nearly 40 years in various publications – including a brief spell as 'Whistle Stop' – the strip seemed to have run its course when Paul moved to America to continue his career.

'It had been wonderful,' says Paul. 'From the very start when I used to get Tottenham manager Bill Nicholson having a go at me for rushing the drawings – I was so busy then I used to do them over a cup of tea and toast, and I sometimes finished them before the toast – to the *Shoot!* years, people just loved it: everyone read them.

'Bobby Moore was always into it, Pat Jennings, Alan Ball, Danny Blanchflower loved it. The only two who were wound up by it were Bill Shankly, who said all these bloody laws were making football soft, and George Best.

'George phoned me once first thing in the morning – he said he'd been out for a run, but really he was just getting

in from the night before – to ask me to draw his "goal" for Northern Ireland against England: he'd nicked the ball away from Gordon Banks as Banks went to clear it and the ref blew for ungentlemanly conduct. He wanted to prove the ref was wrong by getting the drawing in the press.

'I did it, gave it to George – he disappeared and then went and lost it! By that stage George felt he never had the referee protection shown in You Are The Ref. The strips aggravated him. He never stopped reading them though.'

With Paul in the States, 'The Ref' was still fondly remembered and often reprinted, but no more originals were produced. But then, after a gap of nearly 15 years, *The Observer* contacted Paul and Keith to see if they'd be prepared to bring the strip back to life. Both jumped at the chance and, in January 2006, You Are The Ref was reborn.

This unique collection celebrates 50 years of a cult classic. And that turban? It really happened in the 1970s. Find out more on page 77.

THE REF

Keith Hackett, the man in charge of the Premiership's referees, enjoyed a distinguished refereeing career in domestic and international football. He started in 1960 at local level in Sheffield, before moving into the Football League in 1975. He officiated the 1981 FA Cup final and 1985 League Cup final, and ran games at the 1988 European Championship and that year's Olympic Games in Seoul.

It was just after refereeing the 1981 final that I took the call from *Shoot!*. I'd always been an avid reader of You Are The Ref, so being asked to pick up where Clive Thomas – a very good, very controversial referee – left off was a privilege. And more than 20 years later, it feels as fresh as ever.

The feedback we get from the column is overwhelming. There are 30,000 referees in England alone and many have read it since they were kids. It has entertained and educated generations, and it's wonderful for developing knowledge of the laws.

Listening to football phone-ins can be aggravating – hearing callers say 'he was the last man so he should have been sent off', or 'the keeper handled outside the box and all the ref did was award a free-kick' leaves me frustrated.

But knowing we can at least get the message across in these strips has always been a relief. And since it returned – long overdue – in *The Observer*, I'm constantly being stopped by people in the street wanting to debate the previous week's answers, or pose new questions.

I've been involved in the game since 1960. So much has happened in that time – so many great players and great moments. Cast your mind back to the image of George Best making a muddy pitch look like velvet. Remember Bobby Moore and the time he had on the ball; Michel Platini and his subtle passes; Karl-Heinz Rummenigge and his explosive pace; the fabulous Kenny Dalglish, who'd run his socks off all afternoon at Anfield clearly enjoying what he was doing; and one of my favourites, Emlyn Hughes,

who'd always quip 'are you sure son?' when I made a decision. It's wonderful that so many of these greats from the past, as well as today's stars, are immortalised in Paul's art. The way he brings the questions and situations to life is magnificent.

The main message I'd like people to take from this book is this: referees are people with integrity, people who care passionately about the game. When you read these strips – the old ones (with their often out-of-date laws, to add an extra challenge!) and the new – bear in mind that a real referee has a split second to make these decisions, to get them right, watched by thousands, sometimes millions on TV. They do a tremendous job, and they deserve our respect.

THE ARTIST

Born in 1934 in Love Lane, in London's Tottenham, 'Trev' was always going to be an artist. As a schoolboy he was already drawing for comics such as *Eagle* and *TV21*, and as an adult his work has appeared in almost every national newspaper, and in magazines from *NME* to the *Radio Times*. He's also the author and illustrator of more than 20 books, and illustrated the 'Gary Player Golf Class', which appeared in 300 newspapers worldwide and became the largest syndicated sports feature in the world.

Paul spent a large part of his career in the US, working with Mark McCormack at IMG on some of America's biggest brands, and is acclaimed as the finest proponent of comic art realism – an expert in accuracy and movement. Disney animator Milt Neil said it took '20 Disney drawings to produce the movement Trevillion captures in one'.

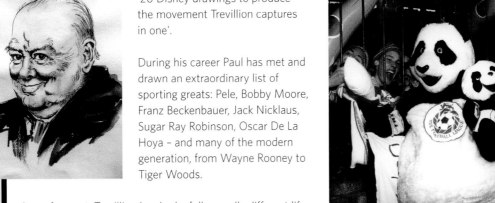

During his career Paul has met and drawn an extraordinary list of sporting greats: Pele, Bobby Moore, Franz Beckenbauer, Jack Nicklaus, Sugar Ray Robinson, Oscar De La Hoya – and many of the modern generation, from Wayne Rooney to Tiger Woods.

Away from art, Trevillion has had a full, proudly different life. Among the highlights: a stand-up career alongside the likes of Tommy Cooper, Norman Wisdom and Bob Monkhouse; a brief record deal; he's been crowned world speed-kissing champion (25,009 in two hours); had coffee with, then drawn, Winston Churchill (the portrait, below left, now hangs in the Bernard Sunley Foundation in London's Berkeley Square); devised a split-handed putting technique; caused trouble by drawing Evonne Goolagong in the nude for *The Sun*; invented sock tags, made famous by Don Revie's Leeds Utd team; and dressed up as DJ Bear, the Panda of Peace (below), in the 1980s – to pacify hooligans and spread love in the game.

This book represents one small part of Trevillion's life and career – but a part he rates as 'the best'. 'It's my life – from a kid up to now. In fact, the only thing I've never done in my career is be a top-class referee, and I still want it. I'm not sure what the retirement age is, but if Keith wants me, he just has to ask.'

HEY, REF!

The early years
1952 - 1969

THE WEEKLY SPORTING REVIEW
FRIDAY, MAY 6, 1955

The WEEKLY SPORTING REVIEW
AND SHOW BUSINESS

Registered at the G.P.O. as a newspaper

No. 828   Friday, May 6, 1955   Price 6d. In America 20 cents

19 55
NEWCASTLE UNITED v MANCHESTER CITY
CUP FINAL

JIMMY SCOULAR
NEWCASTLE UTD
CAPTAIN

ROY PAUL
MANCHESTER CITY
CAPTAIN

SPECIALLY DRAWN FOR "WEEKLY SPORTING REVIEW" by 'TREV'

Starting A Rumpus

Our picture shows HANS STRETZ, left, tangling with JOHNNY SULLIVAN, at Belle Vue, but it doesn't show the rumpus that started in round nine and continued until some time after the end. Read the ringside account of the bout on pages 8 and 9.

HEY, REF!

● The crowd cheered as Brian Plough hit a terrific shot for goal. But the referee was in direct line, and the ball sent him spinning to the ground in an unconscious heap. Luckily for Plough, the ball rebounded to his feet and he promptly slammed it into the net.

● The goalkeeper made no attempt to save. He pointed to the unconscious referee and claimed that play should have stopped immediately the referee was in no condition to officiate. WHAT'S THE VERDICT?

Peter BROADBENT Wolves

LEFT: The Weekly Sporting Review and Show Business, Friday 6 May 1955. Preview to the next day's FA Cup final: Newcastle 3 (Milburn 1, Mitchell 53, Hannah 60), Manchester City 1 (Johnstone 44). The official Wembley attendance: 100,000.

¿ SPORTS QUIZ ?

1 GIVE THE COMPLETE TEST MATCH RECORD OF SIR DON BRADMAN

2 WHICH TEAM WON THE F.A. CUP IN 1921 ?

3 WHEN WERE BOXING GLOVES FIRST USED ?

4 HOW MANY BALLS COMPRISE A SNOOKER SET?

5 HOW MANY TIMES HAS "SUGAR" RAY ROBINSON TAKEN THE FULL COUNT ?

6 WHAT IS THE HEIGHT OF A LAWN TENNIS NET AT THE CENTRE ?

7 WHICH JOCKEY HOLDS THE RECORD FOR THE MOST WINS IN SUCCESSION ?

8 CAN A BOXER LEAVE THE RING DURING THE INTERVAL BETWEEN ROUNDS ?

9 WHAT IS THE HIGHEST SCORE RECORDED IN AN INTERNATIONAL FOOTBALL MATCH ?

10 WHICH CRICKETER HOLDS THE RECORD FOR THE FASTEST CENTURY ?

P. TREVILLION/58

SPORTS QUIZ ANSWERS

1—Tests 52; Runs 6,996; 100's 29; 50's 13; Ave. 99.94; Wickets 2; Ave. 36.00; Catches 32.

2—Tottenham Hotspur.

3—1818.

4—22.

5—Never.

6—3 feet.

7—Sir Gordon Richards (G.B.) won the last race on October 3, 1933, all the six next day and the first five on October 5 — total twelve. This was equalled last week by Pieter Phillipus Stroebel, Phodesian jockey.

8—No. If a boxer did, his departure would be ruled by the referee as a retirement.

9—17. This occurred in the England v Australia Test match at Sydney in 1951 when England won 17-nil.

10—35 minutes — P. G. H. Fender, Surrey v Northamptonshire, at Northampton, 1920.

HEY, REF!

IT'S A GOAL! F.A. Law 5 states the goal should be allowed if, in the opinion of the linesman nearer to the incident, the goal was properly scored.

AND NOW?
How the answers have changed: 5) Robinson was never knocked out, though did suffer one technical knockout. 9) In 2001 Australia beat American Samoa 31-0 in a World Cup qualifier at Coffs Harbour, New South Wales. Archie Thompson scored an international record 13 goals. 10) Wisden still recognises Fender's record, by discounting faster centuries set off 'declaration bowling'.

Danny
BLANCHFLOWER
Spurs

SPORTS QUIZ ?

1. [portrait]

2. WHEN WAS THE SCOTTISH LEAGUE FORMED?

3. WHO WON THE MEN'S SINGLE'S WORLD TABLE TENNIS TITLE IN 1949?

4. HOW MANY WINNERS DID FRED ARCHER RIDE DURING HIS CAREER?

DID FREDDIE MILLS EVER WIN A WORLD TITLE?

5. NAME THE FIRST SOUTH PAW BOXER TO WIN A WORLD TITLE

7. WHEN WAS THE WHITE BALL FIRST USED OFFICIALLY IN FOOTBALL?

6. HAVE THE ENGLISH CRICKET BOWLING AVERAGES EVER BEEN TOPPED BY AN AMERICAN?

9. ON WHICH CRICKET GROUND WAS THE FIRST EVER TEST MATCH PLAYED IN ENGLAND?

8. WHICH PLAYER TOOK PART IN THE FIRST £10,000 TRANSFER FEE?

10. NAME THE FIRST ENGLISHMAN TO WIN THE WORLD SPEEDWAY CHAMPIONSHIP

P.TREVILLION /58

Sports Quiz Answers

1. Yes! Beat Gus Lesnevich for World Light - heavy weight title at White City in 1948.
2. 1891.
3. Johnny Leach.
4. Won 2,748 out of 8,084 races including 5 Derbys and 6 St. Legers.
5. Al McCoy who took the World Middleweight title by knocking out George Chip in one round at Brooklyn on April 7, 1914.
6. For the first and only time the English bowling averages were headed by an American J. B. King, a fast bowler who took 87 wickets for 11.01 runs each (year 1908).
7. 1951.
8. 1928. First £10,000 transfer fee: paid by Arsenal for David Jack of Bolton Wanderers.
9. Kennington Oval (England v. Australia, 1880).
10. Tommy Price (Wembley) in 1949.

Soccer Sketchbook—7

● Seamus O'Toole was a brilliant football captain, but he always had difficulty controlling his Irish temper. And he was flaming mad when he lost the toss and realised he would have to play facing the sun.

● The referee blew his whistle for the game to begin. But at that very moment O'Toole shook everyone by racing to the opposing skipper and hitting him with a hefty right under the chin. The referee had no hesitation in ordering O'Toole off the field. Seamus shrugged his shoulders and told the referee that he would send out a replacement. What's the verdict?

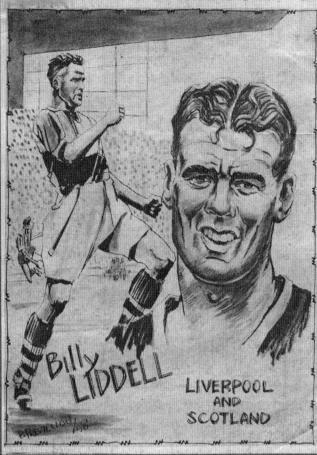

Billy LIDDELL

LIVERPOOL AND SCOTLAND

THE SPACE AGE

TOTTENHAM 2 BLACKPOOL 3

SPURS KICKED OFF WITH A BANG AND SMITH RELEASED THE FIRST ROCKET OF THE MATCH TO PUT SPURS ONE UP.

I'M AN AMERICAN ROCKET

BLACKPOOL HIT BACK AND TED, MOVING LIKE A GREEN SATELLITE, BROUGHT THE HOUSE DOWN WITH A SUPERB SAVE.

PROVING IT WAS NOT ALL SPACE STUFF MAESTRO STAN PICKED UP A PERFECT DITCHBURN PASS AND SENT UP ONE FOR CHARNLEY TO FIRE HOME.

SECOND HALF

BLACKPOOL, FIRST TO ADJUST THEIR SIGHTS, SEND ROCKET N°2 PAST TED.

TOTTENHAM WASTED NO TIME AND WERE SOON BACK ON LEVEL TERMS — BUT GOALKEEPER FARM WAS RELUCTANT TO RETURN THE BALL, PERHAPS HE THOUGHT IT WAS A SPACE HELMET.

MINUTES LATER MUDIE UNLEASHED BLACKPOOL'S 3RD ROCKET AND LAST GOAL OF THE MATCH TO GIVE BLACKPOOL BOTH POINTS.

I SUGGEST TOTTENHAM, WHO TWICE HIT THE BAR IN THE CLOSING MINUTES, SHOULD TAKE A FEW LESSONS FROM THE YANKS ON HOW TO KEEP THEIR ROCKETS DOWN.

Len WHITE

NEWCASTLE

Centre-forward, inside-forward or winger — all positions come alike to Newcastle's LEN WHITE.

INTRODUCING— Every week throughout the soccer season the "Weekly Herald" will be publishing a cartoon featuring soccer stars in action and incidents from the matches. They will be by Paul Trevillion, a young artist whose work is featured regularly in national sporting periodicals. On Saturday he was at White Hart Lane complete with sketch pad and pencil, for the opening game of the season with Blackpool. As well as covering home matches he will also be travelling to many of the Spurs away matches, his keen eye and skilful hand capturing those little details which even a camera cannot record.

HEY, REF!

● O'Toole was right. The rules state that if a player is sent off the field before a game actually begins another player may take his place, though the kick-off must not be delayed.

23 August 1958

Tommy
DOCHERTY
(Arsenal)

P. TREVILLION
58

HEY, REF!

DANNY CAULIFLOWER is playing for the reserve team; but at half-time he hears that his first team. who are playing near by. have only ten men and are 2—0 down.

A real hero is Danny. He borrows a motor-scooter and dashes off to the aid of the first team. He plays a blinder . . . until he tells his story to an opposing player who complains to the referee.

What's the verdict?

Answer at foot of column 4

TOMMY DOCHERTY, Arsenal's new £25,000 left-half from Preston, has proved the lynch-pin in the new-look Arsenal team.

Scottish international Docherty has given the side the punch that was lacking in early matches, and his co-operation with his forwards has brought a lot of goals to the club.

ALUN
WILLIAMS
Bristol
CITY

ALUN WILLIAMS, the Bristol City centre-half, is fast making a name for himself as a cool and constructive defender. Winner of Football League and Association representative honours, Bristol - born Williams has the ability and the confidence to win even greater honours.

BLACK-OUT

TOTTENHAM 2 LEEDS 3

IT WAS CERTAINLY A DARK DAY FOR THE SPURS FANS, THE ONLY BRIGHT SPOT BEING THE AMPLE DOME OF REFEREE W. CLEMENTS.

DRESSED IN THE LATEST FASHION WITH HIS CLEANEST CLEAN AND SNOWY WHITE COLLAR AND CUFFS

HE MADE MORE NOISE IN THE FIRST HALF THAN ALL THE SPURS FANS PUT TOGETHER.

IN THE SECOND HALF OUR REFEREE FRIEND WAS CALLED UPON TO MAKE MANY HAIR LINE DECISIONS.

AND EVERYONE AGREED THAT THIS WAS INDEED A GENEROUS ACT.

IN FACT OUR Mr CLEMENTS WAS UNDOUBTEDLY THE BIGGEST STAR OF THIS MATCH IN MORE WAYS THAN ONE

TREVILLION

25 October 1958

HEY, REF!

DANNY should have kept his mouth shut! He is ordered off under F.A Law No. 3, which states that a player who leaves a match before it is completed must not take part in another game.

SPORTS QUIZ ?

1)

2) WHO WAS THE FIRST IRISHMAN TO WIN THE OPEN GOLF CHAMPIONSHIP?

3)

4) WHEN WERE THE TWO BAILS FIRST USED IN COUNTY CRICKET?

WHO WAS THE OLDEST HEAVYWEIGHT TO WIN THE WORLD TITLE?

5)

6) WHO WAS THE FIRST FOOTBALLER TO BE TRANSFERRED FOR A FOUR-FIGURE FEE?

DID SAM BARTRAM EVER RECEIVE A FULL INTERNATIONAL CAP?

WHICH BOWLER HOLDS THE RECORD FOR THE BEST INNINGS ANALYSIS?

7)

8) NAME THE SMALLEST HORSE TO WIN THE DERBY

9)

WHICH CRICKETER HOLDS THE RECORD FOR THE MOST CATCHES IN A SEASON?

NAME THE TWO CLUBS WHO HAVE WON THE FIRST DIVISION CHAMPIONSHIP IN THREE SUCCESSIVE SEASONS

10) WHO WAS THE HEAVIEST BOXER TO WIN THE WORLD TITLE?

P. TREVILLION/58

Ron WYLIE Aston Villa

TREV 59.

Answers to Sports Quiz

1.—"Jersey" Walcot 37½.
2.—Fred Daly in 1947.
3.—No. Only war-time caps.
4.—1816.
5.—10 wickets for 10 runs— H. Verity in 1932.
6.—When Sunderland transferred A. Common to Middlesbrough in 1905 for a £1,000 fee.
7.—Huddersfield and Arsenal. Huddersfield in the seasons 1923-4, 1924-5, 1925-6. Arsenal in the seasons 1932-3, 1933-4, 1934-5.
8.—"Little Wonder" the 1840 winner, stood only 14 hand 3½ inches.
9.—W. R. Hammond, 78 (1928).
10.—Primo Carnera — 19 st. 4 lb.

HEY, REF!

WHAT a shot! The goalkeeper could only stare as this crashing drive from centre-forward Ralph Barter smashed against the cross-bar with such force that it broke it clean off. Barter pounced on the rebound and banged it in again. The goalkeeper made no attempt to save. He just pointed to the wrecked cross-bar and appealed to the referee.

HEY, REF!

IT'S a goal. F.A. Law 10 states that if a cross-bar becomes displaced during a game the referee should award a goal if, in his opinion, the ball crosses the goal-line at a point where the cross-bar should have been

? SPORTS · QUIZ ?

② WHICH FAMOUS SPORTING FIGURE WAS KNOWN AS THE RUSSIAN LION?

③ WHO WAS THE FIRST BLACK BOXER TO WIN A WORLD CHAMPIONSHIP

④ WHICH FOOTBALL CLUB HAS WON BOTH THE F.A. CUP AND F.A. AMATEUR CUP?

⑤ NAME THE COUNTY WHICH HAS A RECORD OF MORE THAN 200 RUNS FOR EACH WICKET PARTNERSHIP

⑥ NAME THE ONLY ENGLISHWOMAN TO HAVE WON THE U.S. LAWN TENNIS SINGLES TITLE

① SIR LEONARD HUTTON'S 364 RUNS SCORED AT THE OVAL IN 1938 IS STILL THE HIGHEST IN TEST CRICKET. HOW LONG DID THIS INNINGS LAST?

⑦ WHICH FAMOUS BOXER WAS BURIED IN WESTMINSTER ABBEY?

⑧ GIVE THE NAME OF THE OLDEST FOOTBALL LEAGUE CLUB

⑨ HOW MANY TIMES HAS THE OXFORD AND CAMBRIDGE BOAT RACE ENDED IN A DEAD-HEAT?

⑩ WHO SCORED THE FIRST TEST CENTURY FOR ENGLAND?

P TREVILLION

Did You Get the Answers?

(From Page 4)

1—13 hours and 20 minutes.
2—Hackenschmidt, a Russian wrestler.
3—Bantamweight — George Dixon in 1890.
4—Old Carthusians — F.A. Cup in 1881; F.A. Amateur Cup in 1894 and 1897.
5—Essex.
6—Betty Nuthall, 1930.
7—John Broughton.
8—Notts County, 1862.
9—Once, 1877.
10—W. G. Grace; 152 at The Oval, 1880.

HE WAS WRONG

THE following letter has been received from cartoonist P. P. Trevillion, compiler of the popular "Sports Quiz":

"My apologies for slipping up when stating that Hutton's 364, at the Oval in 1938, was still a Test record.

"It was, of course, beaten by Garfield Sobers (West Indies) and I overlooked this in compiling the quiz. I guarantee I will not be caught out on any fact, however insignificant, in the future."

Apology accepted — and thanks to all the readers who wrote pointing out the error. Another Sports Quiz soon.— Editor.

AND NOW?
How the answers have changed: 1) Sobers' record 365 against Pakistan eventually fell to Brian Lara's 375 against England in 1994. Lara has since recaptured his record from Matthew Hayden with 400. 6) Virginia Wade won the US Open in 1968.

HEY, REF!

● A real Rovers fanatic is Bill Sofat, and he's positive this is the year his side will win the Cup.

But it's a bad omen for Bill when a lob shot sails over the stranded Rovers 'keeper towards the empty net. That's when Bill jumped the barrier and threw himself at the ball. But he was too late—the ball goes over the line.

Nevertheless, the Rovers goal-keeper appeals to the referee. What's the verdict?

Frank BLUNSTONE
Chelsea

HEY, REF!

Too bad, Bill. It's a goal. F.A. laws state that if a spectator tries to prevent a goal, but fails to make contact with the ball—it must be a goal.

The Liverpool Echo and Evening Express, Saturday 17 December 1960.
Celebration of that season's successful Everton side.

STANLEY MATTHEWS
BLACKPOOL & ENGLAND

GILBERT MERRICK
BIRMINGHAM & ENGLAND

BRIAN PILKINGTON
BURNLEY & ENGLAND

Soccer Sketchbook—11

Peter McPARLAND
ASTON VILLA
AND
IRELAND

P. TREVILLION/58

SPORTS QUIZ ?

1. WHO HOLDS THE RECORD FOR THE LONGEST REIGN AS WORLD HEAVYWEIGHT CHAMPION ?

2. WHEN DID THE BRILLIANT STANLEY MATTHEWS FIRST PLAY FOR STOKE, AND HOW MUCH DID HE COST THE CLUB ?

3. WHICH BOWLER HOLDS THE RECORD FOR THE MOST WICKETS IN A MATCH ?

4. WHICH TEAMS WON THE F.A. CUP IN THREE SUCCESSIVE SEASONS ?

5. WHO WAS THE FIRST MAN TO SWIM THE CHANNEL ?

6. WHO HOLDS THE RECORD FOR THE GREATEST NUMBER OF DERBY WINS ?

7. WHICH RUGBY PLAYER HOLDS THE RECORD FOR THE GREATEST NUMBER OF CONVERSIONS IN A SEASON ?

8. WHO WAS THE LIGHTEST HEAVYWEIGHT TO WIN THE WORLD CROWN ?

9. HOW MANY HORSES HAVE WON ALL FIVE CLASSIC RACES ?

10. WHAT IS THE HIGHEST "BENEFIT" EVER ACCORDED A CRICKETER ?

P. TREVILLION/58

P TREV '58
Tommy JOHNSTON (Blackburn)

Busby Babe

WILF McGUINNESS
MANCHESTER UNITED

SPORTS QUIZ ANSWERS

1—Joe Louis. 11 years 8 months 9 days.

2—1931-2. Cost to the club was £10 signing-on fee.

3—J. C. Laker took 19 wickets for 90 runs (9-37 and 10-53) for England v Australia, at Manchester in 1956.

4—Wanderers (London) in 1875-76, 1876-77, 1877-78 and Blackburn Rovers in 1883-4, 1884-5, 1885-6.

5—Capt. Matthew Webb (G.B.) 24-25, August, 1875.

6—G. Robinson won six times: 1817, 1824, 1825, 1827, 1828 and 1836.

7—J. Sullivan (Wigan) 200 in 1933-34.

8—Bob Fitzsimmons, 11 stone, 13 lbs.

9—None.

10—£14,000 C. Washbrook (Lancashire) in 1948.

I REGRET that in a recent Sports Quiz I named Jim Sullivan as holder of the record for the greatest number of conversions in a rugby season.

As many readers have pointed out, Sullivan's total of 200 was beaten last season by B. Ganley (Oldham) with 228.
—P. TREVILLION, Hornsey, London, N.

● *Hope this appeases all you irate Oldham fans.*

AND NOW?
How the answers have changed: 6) Lester Piggott won the Derby nine times. 7) David Watkins struck 221 conversions for Salford in 1972-73. 10) Benefits regularly exceed £100,000. Reports claim that Andrew Flintoff will receive more than £1million, possibly even £3m, for his.

SPORTS QUIZ ?

1. WHAT IS THE HIGHEST NUMBER OF KNOCKDOWNS RECORDED IN A WORLD TITLE BOUT?

2. GIVE THE TOTAL NUMBER OF RACES WON BY SIR GORDON RICHARDS

3. HOW MANY CLUBS HAVE WON BOTH THE F.A. CUP AND PROMOTION IN THE SAME SEASON?

4. WHAT IS THE RECORD FOR THE HIGHEST NUMBER OF CONSECUTIVE MAIDEN OVERS BOWLED?

5. WHAT IS THE TIME FOR THE FASTEST CENTURY BREAK IN BILLIARDS?

6. WHAT IS THE GREATEST NUMBER OF RUNS SCORED IN A SINGLE DAY?

7. WHO TOOK PART IN THE FIRST WORLD HEAVYWEIGHT TITLE FIGHT WITH GLOVES?

8. WHO WAS THE YOUNGEST EVER CHAMPION AT WIMBLEDON?

9. WHAT IS THE RECORD TIME FOR SWIMMING THE CHANNEL?

10. WHAT IS THE SMALLEST WINNING MARGIN OF A UNIVERSITY BOAT RACE?

P TREVILLION 58

Answers to Sports Quiz

1—Max Baer knocked down Primo Carnera 12 times in 11 rounds in their heavyweight title fight in New York on June 14, 1934, before the referee stopped the fight.

2—4,870.

3—One - West Bromwich Albion in 1931. Promotion from 2nd Division.

4—17. By H. L. Hazell for Somerset v Gloucestershire at Taunton in 1949.

5—On October 10, 1952, Walter Lindrum (Australia) made a 100 break in 27.5 seconds.

6—721 runs (10 wickets) by the Australians against Essex in 1948.

7—The first world heavyweight title fight, with gloves, was on September 7, 1892, between John L. Sullivan and James J. Corbett in New Orleans, U.S.A.

8—Miss Charlotte Dodd who was 15 when she won in 1887.

9—10 hrs. 50 mins. by the Egyptian Hassan Abd - el - Rheim on August 22, 1950.

10—By a canvas in 1952. Oxford won.

HEY, REF!

● Attempting to clear a swerving centre City's left-back collided with the goalpost and was knocked out and carried off the field. With only ten men, City's defence was completely overrun.

● Rovers' right-winger, George Johns, received a pass and broke through on his own. But at that moment City's injured left-back sensed the danger, poked his foot on the field of play and tripped the unfortunate Johns. What's the verdict?

P TREVILLION 59

AND NOW?
How the answers have changed: 1) The original answer was already out of date! In a bantamweight bout in Johannesburg in 1950 Danny O'Sullivan was knocked down by Vic Toweel 14 times in 10 rounds. 4) RG Nadkarni bowled 21 consecutive maidens for India against England in the Madras Test of 1963-64. 9) The fastest ever verified swim of the channel was by Christof Wandratsch in 2005. He crossed the channel in 7 hours 3 minutes and 52 seconds. The fastest swim of the channel made under Channel Swimming Association rules is by Chad Hundeby of the USA on the 27th September 1994. He crossed the channel in 7 hours 17 minutes. 10) Oxford won the 2003 race by one foot.

HEY, REF!

● It's a penalty. . . . F.A. Law 12 states that a penalty must be given, since the offence occurred within the field of play.

SPORT EXPRESS, May 2, 1957.

Sport EXPRESS

6 D.

THE INDEPENDENT SPORTS JOURNAL

Vol. 19, No. 480 - - - MAY 2, 1957

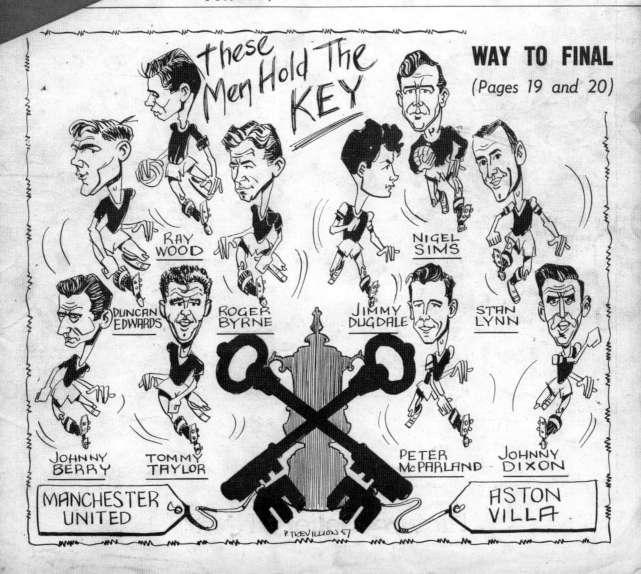

These Men Hold The KEY

WAY TO FINAL
(Pages 19 and 20)

RAY WOOD

NIGEL SIMS

DUNCAN EDWARDS

ROGER BYRNE

JIMMY DUGDALE

STAN LYNN

JOHNNY BERRY

TOMMY TAYLOR

PETER McPARLAND

JOHNNY DIXON

MANCHESTER UNITED

ASTON VILLA

P. TREVILLION 57

**Sport Express, Thursday 2 May 1957. Preview to the FA Cup final,
played two days later: Aston Villa 2 (McParland 68, 73),
Manchester United 1 (Taylor 83). The official Wembley attendance: 100,000.**

Unable to pick up a pen for several days after catching his right thumb in a railway carriage door, cartoonist Paul Trevillion nevertheless managed to rush this Cup-Tie cartoon to the "Weekly Herald." It was produced with his thumb still badly swollen.

10 January 1959, FA Cup third round preview: Tottenham 2 West Ham 0.

★ Charlie Bloggs was always in trouble and every time he went into a tackle he was pulled up for some infringement. But Charlie kept his head—until half-time.

As the referee blew his whistle Charlie raced over to him and told him what he thought of him. But to Charlie's astonishment he was ordered off the field.

Bloggs said it couldn't be done as the game was dead until half-time expired. What's the verdict? See foot of Column Three.

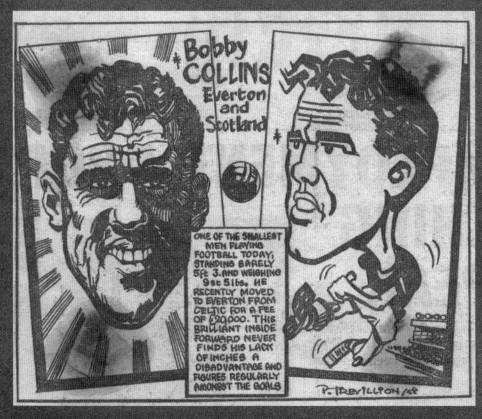

Bobby COLLINS Everton and Scotland

ONE OF THE SMALLEST MEN PLAYING FOOTBALL TODAY; STANDING BARELY 5Ft. 3. AND WEIGHING 9st. 5lbs, HE RECENTLY MOVED TO EVERTON FROM CELTIC FOR A FEE OF £20,000. THIS BRILLIANT INSIDE FORWARD NEVER FINDS HIS LACK OF INCHES A DISADVANTAGE AND FIGURES REGULARLY AMONGST THE GOALS

John BOND West Ham

HEY, REF!

THE ref. was right! F.A. law 3 states that if a player behaves in an ungentlemanly manner during the interval he shall be debarred from taking further part in the match and shall not be replaced.

COACH BUT NO DRIVER !

BILLY NICHOLSON, who has been appointed coach to 'Spurs' Spurlets, will probably not be seen in the Tottenham colours this season. But if Bill can enthuse into the youngsters the same 90 minute endeavour and go-ahead, never-say-die spirit which always characterised his own play; then the 'Spurs will have good reason for satisfaction.

★

Billy Nicholson

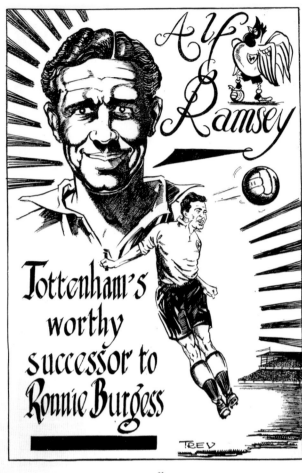

Alf Ramsey

Tottenham's worthy successor to Ronnie Burgess

TREV

21

Artwork from The Lilywhite, 1952-54, where the Hey Ref! idea was conceived.

Tim COLEMAN
STOKE

Ken BROWN WEST HAM

P. TREVILLION 59

Often an unsung hero—West Ham centre-half KEN BROWN. The big fellow has been a key player in West Ham's rise to the top half of the First Division.

Roy SHINER SHEFFIELD WEDNESDAY

TREV 59

ROY SHINER'S all-out, goal-scoring displays have had much to do with Sheffield Wednesday's quick return to the First Division.

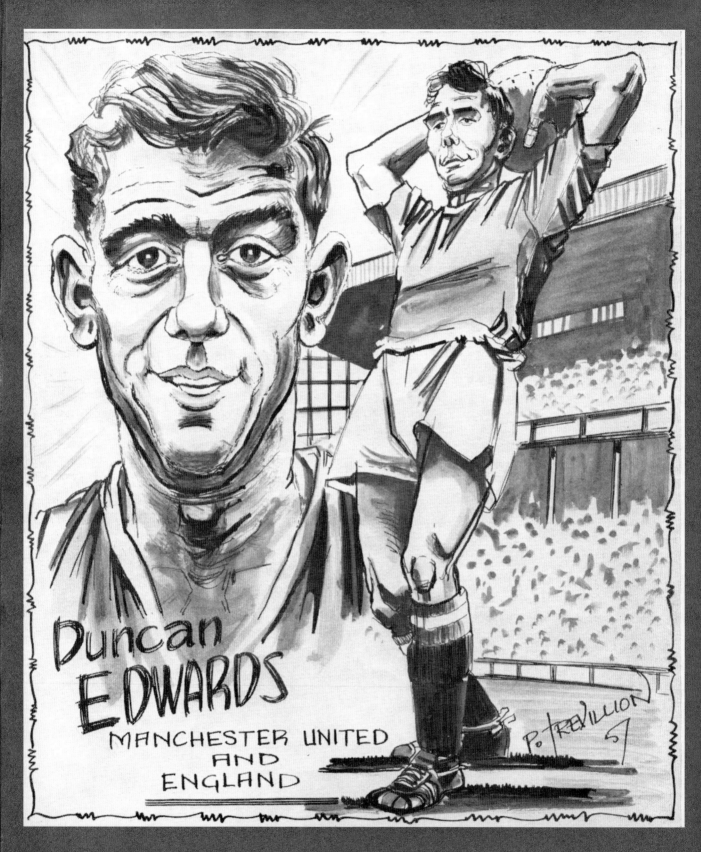

Duncan
EDWARDS
MANCHESTER UNITED
AND
ENGLAND

P. TREVILLION 57

A 1957 original which was published as part of the Soccer Sketchbook series.
Edwards died in the Munich air disaster the following year, aged 21.

HEY, REF!

● *Billy Bright is famed for his long throws-in. It's a piece of cake for him to throw half-way across the field.*

● *In one game he was called to take a throw-in from near the corner flag in his own half. Billy made it a long one —back to his own goalkeeper.*

● *Unfortunately, the 'keeper missed it and the ball bounced gently into the net. Was it a goal?*

DAZZLED

SPURS 5. PRESTON 1.

SPURS GOT OFF TO A GREAT START WITH A CLIFF JONES' GOAL IN THE FIRST FEW MINUTES →

BUT PRESTON, LED BY BRILLIANT Tom Finney → HIT BACK TO EQUALISE

AND ALTHOUGH Finney CONTINUED TO DAZZLE HE WAS THE ONE WHO LEFT THE FIELD DAZED BY A HEAD INJURY

Finney-less PRESTON SOON FOUND THEMSELVES BEHIND IN THE SECOND HALF

GOAL!

AND IT WAS NO SURPRISE TO SEE PRESTON, WHO FINISHED WITH ONLY 9 MEN, LOSE 5-1

What a carry on!

You mean 'OFF!

WHAT A PITY THE PRESTON GOAL NEVER GOT INJURED — AT LEAST IT WOULD HAVE MADE THINGS A LITTLE MORE EVEN

Another 3 yards of bandage, George!

TREVILLION 59

19 September 1959

Albert QUIXALL

Noel CANTWELL West Ham.

TREV 59

Star Attacker

Ernie TAYLOR SUNDERLAND

ERNIE TAYLOR, the former Newcastle, Blackpool, Manchester United and England inside - forward, has done much to ease Sunderland's relegation worries.

HEY, REF...

● *No goal. Football Association Law 15 states the referee must award a corner kick.*

Spurs take on Newport in the FA Cup fourth round, January 1959.

GIANT KILLERS

EVERY YEAR THE CUP SEES A GIANT KILLER AND THIS YEAR NEWPORT ARE ALL SET TO TAKE THAT LABEL

I'm alright JACK

HAVING COMPILED A HOST OF PLANS FOR SPURS DOWNFALL

AND IF PLAN 68 FAILS AS WELL WE MAY EVEN TRY PLAYING FOOTBALL

THEIR CAPTAIN ALF SHERWOOD IS MORE THAN CONFIDENT HIS BOYS WILL GO INTO THE HAT FOR THE NEXT ROUND

AND AFTER SPURS LET'S HAVE WOLVES WE DON'T WANT PEOPLE SAYING WE HAD AN EASY RUN TO WEMBLEY

BUT TOTTENHAM ENSURED THAT THERE WILL BE NO GIANT KILLING ACT THIS SATURDAY. THEY HAVE SENT OUT MANAGER BILLY NICHOLSON FOR ELEVEN JARS OF SLIMMING PILLS.

F.A. CUP 5TH ROUND

REDUCING PILLS FOR GIANTS

TREVILLION 59

IN STEP

TOTTENHAM. 4 NEWPORT. 1

TOTTENHAM KICKED OFF DETERMINED TO WIN AND SO TAKE THE NEXT STEP TO WEMBLEY, BUT NEWPORT PROVED TO BE NO WALK-OVER

DUNMORE RACED OFF WITHOUT WAITING FOR THE NEWPORT AMBER TO TURN GREEN AND SLAMMED IN SPURS FIRST GOAL

GOAL

AND ALTHOUGH NEWPORT HIT BACK ANOTHER DUNMORE SPECIAL CLOSE ON HALF-TIME SAW SPURS STEP OFF 2 UP

TOTTENHAM STARTED THE SECOND HALF DREAMING WHO THEY WERE GOING TO MEET IN THE NEXT ROUND

IT TOOK A NEWPORT GOAL TO BRING THEM BACK TO EARTH

SKIPPER SMITH (A HOSPITAL PATIENT DURING THE WEEK) GAVE THE SPURS FANS A DOSE OF JUST WHAT THE DOCTOR ORDERED WHEN HE SLAMMED IN TWO LATE GOALS FOR A 4-1 SPURS WIN

NEXT

N.B. 4 WINS ON THE TROT SPURS HAVE FOUND THEIR FEET IN TIME FOR THE HARD ROAD TO WEMBLEY

TREVILLION 59

HEY, REF!

LOOKS like a spot of trouble here for Rovers centre-forward Charlie Smith when he refuses to kick-off for the second half. It was a cold day and the referee decided to allow only three minutes break for half-time, but Charlie insisted on five minutes and wouldn't budge until the time was up.

★

His action resulted in the referee ordering him off the field for ungentlemanly conduct. Who was right?

Bunny LARKIN Birmingham

TREVILLION 59

HEY, REF!

CHARLIE was right F.A. Laws state that players are entitled to an interval of five minutes at half-time.

Football Facts and Figures
RESULTS AND LINE-UPS FOR SATURDAY, APRIL 27

FIRST DIVISION

Aston Villa .. (0) 1   Luton .... (0) 3
Smith   Turner (2), Brown
                                27,000

Birmingham .. (2) 3   Manchester C. (1) 3
Brown,   Kirkman (2),
Phoenix (o.g.),   Hall (o.g.)
Govan   23,700

Bolton ...... (1) 1   Everton ...... (0) 1
Lofthouse   Temple   16,016

Cardiff ...... (0) 2   Manchester U. (1) 3
Hitchens (2)   Scanlon (2, 1 a pen.),
                       McSeveney (o.g.)
                                18,000

Portsmouth .. (0) 0   West Brom. .. (0) 1
                       Allen   24,065

Preston ...... (1) 1   Chelsea ...... (0) 0
Hatsell   13,592

Tottenham .. (1) 2   Blackpool .... (0) 1
Harmer (2, 1 a pen.) Mudie   49,878

SECOND DIVISION

Bristol C. .... (1) 3   Swansea .... (0) 1
Curtis (3)   Peake   19,104

L. Orient .... (2) 2   Notts C. .... (2) 2
Johnston, Andrews   Wills (2)   12,321

Lincoln ...... (2) 4   Barnsley .... (0) 1
Linnecor (2),   Holmes   7,295
Northcott, Smillie

Liverpool .... (0) 1   West Ham .. (0) 0
Liddell (pen.)   36,236

Port Vale .... (1) 2   Rotherham .. (1) 1
Leake (2)   Farmer   7,038

Sheffield U. .. (0) 0   Nottingham F. (1) 4
                       Lishman (3),
                       Wilson   28,103

Sport Express, 1957

Soccer Sketchbook—4

Bobby CHARLTON
MANCHESTER UNITED
AND
ENGLAND

Top Quality

THERE are few more consistent centre-halves in the game than Stoke City's Ken Thomson. He cost Stoke over £20,000 when signed from his local club, Aberdeen.

Although missing out on international honours so far, Ken can take pride in the fact that he took over in the Stoke side from English international Neil Franklin and in the eyes of Stoke fans "filled his shoes quite adequately enough."

KEN THOMSON (Stoke)

★ HEY, REF! ★

RON DAYNHAM had quite a shock when he took a goal kick against a strong wind. Though the ball went outside the penalty area it was blown back into the goalmouth.

Daynham juggled with the ball, but it slipped between his legs just over the goal-line. In a flash, Ron retrieved it and kicked the ball down the field. But already the opposing team were appealing for a goal. What's the verdict?

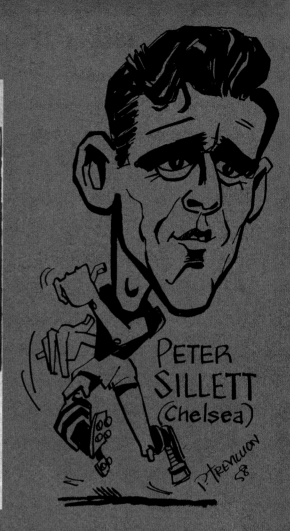

PETER SILLETT (Chelsea)

BILLY WRIGHT (Wolves)

HEY, REF!

"NO goal," said the ref. He followed F.A. Law 16 and awarded an indirect free kick instead.

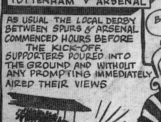

VOCAL DERBY

TOTTENHAM v ARSENAL

AS USUAL THE LOCAL DERBY BETWEEN SPURS & ARSENAL COMMENCED HOURS BEFORE THE KICK-OFF. SUPPORTERS POURED INTO THE GROUND AND WITHOUT ANY PROMPTING IMMEDIATELY AIRED THEIR VIEWS

SPURS FAN — I ONLY WISH THIS WAS THE SEMI-FINAL—WE'D BE CERTS FOR WEMBLEY

THIS CONFIDENT FAN COUNTS HIS CHICKENS EVEN BEFORE THE EGGS ARE LAID—SPURS HAVE STILL TO WIN THROUGH ANOTHER TWO ROUNDS BEFORE THE SEMI-FINAL

ARSENAL FAN — I HAVEN'T TRAVELLED ALL THIS WAY TO SEE THEM LOSE

THIS FAN LOVES TO EXAGGERATE. HIGHBURY TO TOTTENHAM IS AT THE MOST A 45 MINUTE JOURNEY. IN ANY CASE HE'S PROBABLY AN ARSENAL FAN LIVING IN TOTTENHAM

NEUTRAL FAN — IT'S A PITY THEY BOTH CAN'T WIN

THIS FELLA'S A FIBBER—WHY! HE KNOWS FULL WELL HE'S MARKED THIS MATCH A BANKER DRAW.

SCHOOLBOY FAN — MAY THE BEST TEAM WIN

WHAT A WOPPER, HE'S ONLY INTERESTED IN GETTING HOME IN TIME TO SEE HIS FAVOURITE TELEVISION PROGRAMME CHEYENNE

FOOTBALL FAN — WELL I MANAGED TO DODGE THE AFTERNOON SHOPPING

THIS SUPPORTER IS, AT LEAST, TELLING THE TRUTH

HOW WONDERFUL IT IS THAT THESE CHAPS CAN SPEAK THEIR MIND UNCHALLENGED — Poor Tommy DOCHERTY OF ARSENAL WAS GIVEN 14 DAYS SUSPENSION FOR SPEAKING HIS

N.B SPURS LOST 4—1

31 January 1959

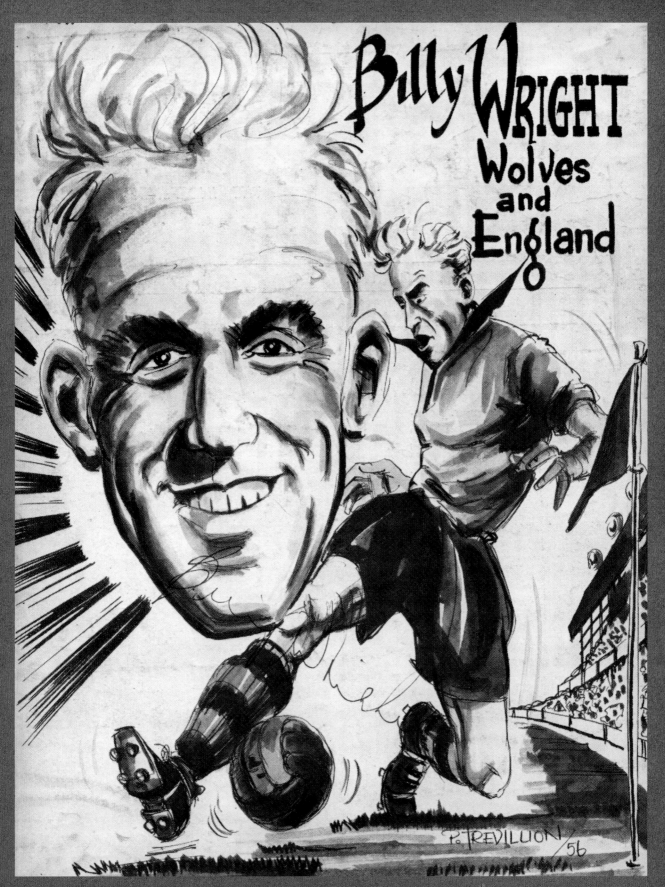

A 1956 original, signed by Billy Wright, which was published as
part of the Soccer Sketchbook series.

HEY, REF!

BILL BLACK, the man in the No. 7 shirt is almost as tricky as Stan Matthews with his body swerves, much to the annoyance of opposing backs. With a neat twist of his body Bill has just glided past the right-back and is all set to score against City.

Undaunted by the goalkeeper's advance, Bill calmly dribbled round him. But in sheer desperation the 'keeper threw himself in a Rugby tackle at Bill's feet and just missed.

As the 'keeper got up he was more than surprised to see the dancing figure of Bill appealing for a penalty. See the referee's verdict in column Three.

The Maestro himself . . . the one and only STANLEY MATTHEWS (who has autographed this drawing by artist TREV)

Soccer Sketchbook—10

Danny CLAPTON
ARSENAL

Nat LOFTHOUSE
BOLTON WANDERERS AND ENGLAND

P. TREVILLION 58

HEY, REF!

IT'S a penalty. F.A. Law 12 states that if a player intentionally trips or attempts to trip an opponent within the penalty area he shall be penalised by a penalty kick.

FIRST DIVISION

Arsenal ...... (2) 3   **Charlton** ..... (0) 1
Holton, Tapscott (2)   Charlton (o.g.)
                               26,364

Birmingham .. (4) 6   **Leeds** ...... (2) 2
Astall, Brown (2),   Charles (2)   30,642
Govan (3, 1 a pen.)

Burnley ...... (0) 0   **Manchester C.** (2) 3
                           Dyson, Clarke,
                           Fagan   16,746

Cardiff ...... (0) 0   **Tottenham** .... (1) 3
                           Dyson, Dunmore,
                           Brooks   30,000

Chelsea ...... (3) 5   **Everton** ...... (0) 1
Brabrook,   Williams   28,317
Saunders (2),
Dunlop (o.g.),
Nicholas

Manchester U. (1) 4   **Sunderland** .. (0) 0
Whelan (2),   58,489
Edwards, Taylor

Newcastle .... (1) 1   **Aston Villa** .. (0) 2
Mitchell   Sewell,
                           McParland   27,850

Portsmouth .. (1) 1   **Wolves** ...... (0) 0
Newman   31,111

Preston ...... (0) 0   **Blackpool** .... (0) 0
                           35,887

Sheffield W. .. (0) 3   **Luton** ...... (0) 0
Quixall (pen.),   22,497
Froggatt, Ellis

West Brom. ... (2) 3   **Bolton** ...... (2) 2
Whitehouse, Kevan,   Stevens, Birch
Robson   17,500

SECOND DIVISION

Bristol R. ..... (0) 0   **Blackburn** .... (1) 1
                           Briggs   20,794

Bury .... (0) 0   **Lincoln** ...... (0) 0
Kelly   9,460

Doncaster .... (2) 4   **Port Vale** .... (0) 0
Tindill (2),   7,626
Cavanagh, Ilkenny

Grimsby ...... (1) 3   **Rotherham** .... (1) 2
Scott (2), Rafferty   Farmer,   13,000
                           Richardson (o.g.)

Huddersfield .. (2) 2   **Swansea** ...... (0) 2
Law, Simpson   Palmer (2)   13,516

Leicester .... (1) 1   **Bristol C.** .... (1) 1
Hines   Curtis   32,653

L. Orient .... (0) 0   **Fulham** ...... (0) 2
                           Stevens (2) 16,436

Liverpool .... (2) 3   **Nottingham F.** (1) 1
Liddell, A'Court,   Barrett   47,671
Rowley

Middlesbrough (1) 3   **Sheffield U.** .. (0) 1
Harris (2 pens.),   Ringstead   25,000
Clough

Notts C. ...... (2) 4   **West Ham** .... (1) 1
Russell, Wills (2),   Smith   17,803
Tucker

Stoke .... (0) 3   **Barnsley** ...... (0) 0
Graver, Bowyer (2)   11,600

Sport Express, 1957

● Looks like another brilliant goal for Johnny Baynes! After dribbling round the advancing goalkeeper, Johnny takes careful aim and slams the ball towards the empty net.

● But at the same time a shaggy dog walks across the face of the goalmouth. There's a terrific yelp as the ball crashes into the dog and sends him bundling into the back of the net. The crowd are certain it's a goal, but what has the referee got to say?

SURPRISE PACKET

NORWICH MANAGER **Archie Macaulay** HAS WIDELY PROCLAIMED THAT HIS TEAM WILL **SURPRISE** SPURS IN THIS WEEKS **CUP MATCH**

IF THAT'S THE CASE TOTTENHAM MUST PREPARE THEMSELVES FOR **ANYTHING**

FOR INSTANCE ......

WILL HE SEND HIS TEAM OUT WEARING **Wyatt Earp** HATS TO MAKE THEM **DEAD SHOTS** IN FRONT OF GOAL

OR WILL HE HAVE **Sabrina** AS CAPTAIN TO GIVE SPURS NEW FOUND CUP FORM AN INFERIORITY COMPLEX

I do feel out of it!

PERHAPS TERRY **DENE** WILL BE IN GOAL FOR IF HE CAN **KEEP OUT** THE ARMY HE CAN **KEEP OUT** ANYTHING

I DAREN'T COMMIT A FOUL, I COULDN'T STAND THE REFEREE GIVING ME MY **MARCHING ORDERS!**

HE MAY EVEN HAVE THEM WEARING THEIR SHIRTS BACK TO FRONT SO SPURS WON'T KNOW IF THEY'RE COMING OR GOING

I'D REALLY FOX THEM IF I RUN BACKWARDS!

BUT THE BIGGEST SURPRISE OF ALL, OF COURSE, WOULD BE IF HE WERE TO INSTRUCT THEM TO BEAT SPURS AT THEIR OWN GAME **FOOTBALL!**

ALL MY LIFE I'VE BEEN KICKED AROUND

TREVILLION

14 February 1959. It finished 1-1 - four days later, Norwich won the replay 1-0.

Graham **SHAW**   SHEFFIELD UNITED

● No goal. Football Association Law 10 states a goal cannot be awarded if the ball comes in contact with any outside agency before passing over the goal line.

Evening Standard

43,103   WEDNESDAY, JANUARY 16, 1963   3d.

SPURS v BURNLEY 4-PAGE SOUVENIR

Here they are . . . the men who aim at knock-out No. 3

SUPER SPURS

BLANCHFLOWER

THE MAN WHO MISSES TODAY'S MATCH—DANNY BLANCHFLOWER! AT 37, DANNY IS THE OLDEST PLAYER IN THE SPURS TEAM. HE WAS TWICE VOTED "FOOTBALLER OF THE YEAR"—A RECORD HE SHARES WITH TOM FINNEY. BORN IN BELFAST, THIS SLIGHTLY BUILT RIGHT-HALF RECEIVED ALL HIS EARLY FOOTBALL TRAINING FROM HIS MOTHER.

TODAY SPURS RUN OUT WITH A DOUBLE AIM—TO KNOCK BURNLEY OUT OF THE CUP FOR THE THIRD YEAR RUNNING—*AND* TO GO ON TO WIN THE TROPHY FOR THE THIRD SUCCESSIVE TIME. CAN EVEN THESE AMAZING SPURS DO THAT? HERE IS THEIR RECORD SO FAR . . .

F.A. CUP WINNERS 1901, 1921, 1961 AND 1962. FIRST DIVISION CHAMPIONS 1951 AND 1961. SECOND DIVISION CHAMPIONS 1920 AND 1950. MOST NOTABLE ACHIEVEMENT—"THE DOUBLE."

TOTTENHAM HOTSPUR BECAME THE FIRST CLUB TO WIN THE CHAMPIONSHIP OF THE LEAGUE AND THE F.A. CUP IN THE SAME SEASON SINCE 1897 WHEN ASTON VILLA LAST PERFORMED THIS FEAT.

BAKER

HENRY

FULL-BACKS PETER BAKER AND RON HENRY DID NOT COST SPURS A PENNY. BAKER MODELS HIMSELF ON FORMER SPURS PLAYER ALF RAMSEY—YES, THE SAME ALF RAMSEY WHO IS NOW ENGLAND'S NEW TEAM MANAGER. HENRY STARTED HIS CAREER AS AN OUTSIDE-LEFT. HE BREEDS PRIZE-WINNING CANARIES IN HIS SPARE TIME.

OF INSIDE-RIGHT JOHN WHITE, FORMER ENGL AND WINGER REG SMITH, WHO WAS WHITE'S MANAGER AT FALKIRK, SAID: "HE IS THE MOST COMPLETE FOOTBALLER I HAVE EVER SEEN." KNOWN THROUGHOUT FOOTBALL AS THE "GHOST," WHITE SNIFFS AMMONIA CAPSULES BEFORE EVERY MATCH TO START HIS BLOOD RACING.

WHITE

AT 6ft - 1½ INCHES, CENTRE-HALF MAURICE NORMAN IS THE TALLEST PLAYER IN THE SPURS TEAM. BEFORE TAKING TO FOOTBALL NORMAN WAS AN EAST ANGLIAN FARMER'S BOY.

NORMAN

MACKAY

LEFT-HALF DAVE MACKAY STARTED LIFE AS A JOINER AND SIGNED PROFESSIONAL FORMS FOR HEARTS ON A TENEMENT STAIRCASE IN EDINBURGH. JOINED SPURS IN 1959 AND IS ACKNOWLEDGED BY ALL AS THE STRONG MAN OF THE SIDE.

MEDWIN

OUTSIDE-RIGHT TERRY MEDWIN HAS BEEN WITH SPURS SIX YEARS. HE IS A FAMILY MAN WITH SIX CHILDREN. *STRANGE NOTE:* WELSH INTERNATIONAL TERRY WAS BORN IN SWANSEA PRISON—IN THE WARDERS' QUARTERS—WHERE HIS FATHER WAS AN OFFICER.

BROWN

AS A SCHOOLBOY, BILL BROWN FANCIED HIMSELF AS AN OUTSIDE-LEFT. BUT WHEN THE SCHOOL GOALKEEPER GOT HURT, BROWN, THE TALLEST BOY IN THE TEAM, WAS POPPED IN GOAL—AND THAT'S WHERE HE STAYED.

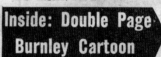

Inside: Double Page Burnley Cartoon

JONES

CLIFF JONES, THE SPURS' LEFT WINGER, IS NATURALLY RIGHT FOOTED—A FACT WHICH OFTEN SURPRISES DEFENDERS. *ODD NOTE:* THE WORLD'S FASTEST WINGER IS LAZY BY NATURE, HE SPENDS ALL HIS SPARE TIME WATCHING TELEVISION.

JOHN SMITH

RESERVE WING-HALF, JOHN SMITH, WAS SIGNED TWO SEASONS AGO FROM WEST HAM IN EXCHANGE FOR DAVE DUNMORE. UNDER-23 CAP SMITH, UNABLE TO COMMAND A REGULAR FIRST-TEAM PLACE AT TOTTENHAM, IS AT PRESENT ON THE TRANSFER LIST.

BOBBY SMITH

AFTER BEING OUT OF THE FIRST ELEVEN FOR FOUR MONTHS, ENGLAND INTERNATIONAL CENTRE-FORWARD BOBBY SMITH CAME BACK WITH A TWO-GOAL BANG AGAINST RANGERS LAST DECEMBER.

Back Page: Jimmy Greaves

LEFT: London Evening Standard, Wednesday 16 January 1963. Preview to Tottenham's FA Cup third round tie. It didn't go according to plan... Spurs lost 3-0 to Burnley at White Hart Lane.

HEY, REF!

CITY full-backs George Sopkins and Harry Dewey are the best of friends off the field, but they are deadly rivals once a game gets under way. They always argue and can never agree.

Even so, it was a big surprise when they started fighting in their own penalty area while the City forwards were attacking strongly in their opponents' half.

The opposing captain lost no time in taking advantage of the incident. He appealed to the referee for a penalty. What's the verdict?

Answer at foot of column 6

Football ECHO

SOUTH WALES ECHO, SAT.

SATURDAY MARCH 19 1966   4d.

Scores—tables

GRAHAM LEGGAT Fulham

DIVISION ONE

Blackburn ..2	Leeds 3	H.T. 0—0
Blackpool ..2	West Ham ..1	H.T. 2—0
Everton 0	Liverpool ..0	H.T. 0—0
Fulham 3	Sunderland ..0	H.T. 3—0
Leicester ..1	Sheffield U. ..0	H.T. 1—0
Man. Utd. ..2	Arsenal 1	H.T. 2—0
Newcastle ..0	Chelsea 1	H.T. 0—0
Notts F. 4	Stoke 3	H.T. 2—3
Sheff. Wed. ..3	N'hampton ..1	H.T. 1—0
Tottenham ..5	Aston Villa ..5	H.T. 4—1
WBA 1	Burnley ..2	H.T. 1—0

	P.	W.	D.	L.	F.	A.	Pts.
Liverpool .	34	22	6	6	68	28	50
Leeds	31	17	8	6	61	29	42
Burnley ..	33	18	6	9	65	41	42
Man. Utd. .	32	15	11	6	63	43	41
Chelsea ..	30	17	5	8	48	37	39
Tottenham	32	14	10	8	67	50	38
Everton ..	35	14	9	12	53	50	37
West Brom.	32	13	9	10	67	54	35
Sheff. Utd.	33	11	11	10	42	48	33
Stoke	32	11	11	10	55	52	33
Leicester ..	30	14	5	11	58	51	33
Arsenal ..	32	10	10	12	51	55	30
West Ham .	33	11	8	14	54	66	30
Aston Villa	33	12	5	16	59	63	29
Notts F. ..	32	11	7	14	44	55	29
Sunderland	33	10	6	17	39	64	26
Sheff. Wed.	30	10	6	14	39	49	26
Newcastle .	32	10	6	16	39	52	26
Nthampton	34	7	10	17	45	80	24
Blackpool	31	8	8	15	40	51	24
Fulham ..	32	8	5	19	48	69	21
Blackburn .	31	7	4	20	50	68	18

DIVISION TWO

Birmingham 0	Bolton W. ..1	H.T. 0—1
Bury 1	Wolves 0	H.T. 1—0
Crystal Pal. ..1	Preston N.E. ..1	H.T. 0—0
Derby 1	Man. City. ..2	H.T. 0—1
Huddersfield .1	Charlton 1	H.T. 1—0
Ipswich 2	Norwich 0	
Leyton Or. ..0	Portsmouth ..0	
Middlesbro. ..0	Plymouth ..1	H.T. 0—1
S'hampton ..1	Rotherham ..1	

	P.	W.	D.	L.	F.	A.	Pts.
Man. City .	32	17	11	4	59	34	45
Huddersfld	43	17	10	6	53	25	44
Coventry ..	32	15	11	6	56	38	41
Bristol C..	33	12	14	7	48	42	38
Wolves ...	33	15	8	10	72	50	38
S'thampton	32	16	6	10	69	47	38
Crystal Pal.	33	13	7	13	38	43	34
Derby	33	13	7	13	53	52	33
Rotherham	31	12	9	10	59	59	33
Plymouth .	33	11	10	12	47	51	32
Birminghm	32	12	7	13	47	54	31
Preston ..	32	9	12	11	44	49	30
Bolton ...	32	12	6	14	42	45	30
Norwich ..	29	9	12	8	39	35	30
Ipswich ..	32	11	7	14	40	47	29
Cardiff C..	31	10	8	13	58	62	28
Carlisle ..	31	12	3	16	44	48	27
Portsmouth	33	7	13	13	54	69	27
Middlesbro'	32	7	12	13	45	60	26
Charlton ..	30	8	10	12	44	55	26
Bury	32	8	7	16	39	52	23
Leyton ..	31	4	9	18	26	60	17

SCOTTISH LEAGUE
Division One

Clyde 6	Dunfermline .1	H.T. 2—0
Dundee Utd. 5	Motherwell ..1	H.T. 1—1
Falkirk 3	Aberdeen 0	H.T. 1—0
Hamilton ..1	Celtic 7	H.T. 1—3
Hibernian ..1	Stirling A. ..0	H.T. 1—0
Kilmarnock ..1	Rangers 1	H.T. 0—0
Morton 0	Hearts 3	H.T. 0—1
Partick Th. ..4	St. Mirren ..1	H.T. 2—1
St. Johnstone 1	Dundee 0	H.T. 1—0

Division Two

Alloa 2	Ayr 1	H.T. 1—1
Berwick 0	Queen's Pk. ..1	H.T. 0—1
Brechin 1	East Fife 3	H.T. 1—2
Dumbarton ..2	Albion 0	H.T. 1—0
Forfar 1	Queen of Sth. 2	H.T. 0—1
Raith Rov. ..3	Montrose ..0	H.T. 2—0
Stranraer ..0	Arbroath 0	H.T. 0—0
Th. Lanark ..0	E. Stirling ..2	H.T. 0—1

HEY, REF!

No penalty. Law 12 states that a referee shall deal with them by caution or dismiss them from the field and award the game to be started with an indirect free kick.

YOU ARE THE REF

35

Soccer Sketchbook—5

Stanley MATTHEWS

BLACKPOOL AND ENGLAND

RIGHT: The Evening Citizen, Saturday 4 May 1963. Preview to the Scottish FA Cup final. It finished 1-1; Rangers won the replay 3-0 11 days later, with two goals from Ralph Brand. Combined attendance for the two games: 249,916.

HEY, REF!

CITY full-backs George Sopkins and Harry Dewey are the best of friends off the field, but they are deadly rivals once a game gets under way. They always argue and can never agree.

Even so, it was a big surprise when they started fighting in their own penalty area while the City forwards were attacking strongly in their opponents' half.

The opposing captain lost no time in taking advantage of the incident. He appealed to the referee for a penalty. What's the verdict?

Peter McPARLAND
Aston Villa

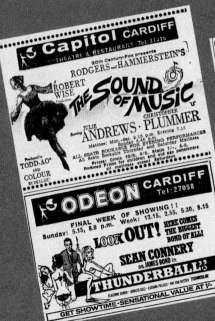

HEY, REF!

No penalty. Law 12 states that a referee shall deal with them by caution or dismiss them from the field and award the game to be started with **an indirect free kick.**

You can rely on
DORMIE
MENSWEAR *Hire* SERVICE
GLASGOW · EDINBURGH · AYR

Evening Citizen

No. 30.870   SATURDAY MAY 4 1963   PRICE 3d

CUP FINAL
SOUVENIR

BELL'S
SCOTCH WHISKY
THE CELEBRATION SCOTCH

RANGERS v CELTIC   1928   1963   THE GREATEST CUP CLASH IN THE WORLD

WHO'LL SCORE THOSE GOLDEN GOALS THIS TIME?

RANGERS	CELTIC
BILLY RITCHIE	(PROBABLE TEAM)
BOBBY SHEARER	FRANK HAFFEY
DAVE PROVAN	DUNCAN MACKAY
JOHN GREIG	JIM KENNEDY
RON McKINNON	JOHN McNAMEE
JIM BAXTER	BILLY McNEILL
WILLIE HENDERSON	BILLY PRICE
GEORGE McLEAN	JIM JOHNSTONE
JIMMY MILLAR	BOBBY MURDOCH
RALPH BRAND	JOHN HUGHES
DAVY WILSON	JOHN DIVERS
	FRANK BROGAN

REFEREE:
TOM WHARTON

Bingo! It's a Millar special!

GIVE JIMMY MILLAR A SIGHT OF GOAL AND ... BINGO! FAST IN THOUGHT AND ACTION JIMMY DOESN'T MISS MANY CHANCES (130 GOALS IN 4 SEASONS). HE'S STRONG — BUT NO BASHER, HARD IN THE TACKLE, HAS TWO GOOD FEET AND IS A GAME "READER" OF A GAME. MILLAR USES THE OPEN SPACE TO ADVANTAGE, PLAYS WELL OFF THE BALL AND PASSES WITH GREAT ACCURACY. OFTEN THE DYNAMIC SPEARHEAD OF THE ATTACK, MILLAR IS EQUALLY EFFECTIVE AT DICTATING THE GAME FROM BEHIND HIS FORWARD LINE.

Big John, the nimble Colossus

"MY JOB IS TO GET THE BALL IN THE NET," SAYS JOHN HUGHES. WITH 31 GOALS LAST SEASON AND OVER 20 THIS TERM, BIG JOHN'S DOING A "GRAND JOB." FAST AND FEARLESS, HE ROARS DOWN THE MIDDLE, REMINISCENT OF THE LEGENDARY JIMMY QUINN. OVER SIX FEET TALL, THIS COLOSSUS FROM COATBRIDGE OFTEN AMAZES WITH HIS DEFT, CLOSE DRIBBLING AND CLEVER BALL CONTROL. TWENTY-YEAR-OLD HUGHES PREFERS TO PLAY AGAINST A BIG CENTRE-HALF. LOOK OUT, RONNIE McKINNON!

The last time . . .

April 14, 1928. There was a jinx on Rangers. For quarter of a century they had failed to win the Cup. And, in the first half, Celtic had completely dominated the play. Then came THAT penalty. It was a moment of truth for Meiklejohn. But Davie accepted his responsibility as captain and took the kick that broke the 25-year hoodoo . . .

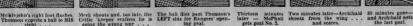

55 MINS. GONE...

Fleming breaks through and has only John Thomson to beat. Willie McStay rushes back . . .

Thomson runs out to block Fleming. McStay covers the goal . . .

Fleming neatly side-steps Thomson and blasts the ball for goal . . .

The perfect shot looks net-bound, but McStay punches clear . . .

Hampden erupts. It's a penalty.

Meiklejohn's right foot flashes. Thomson expects a ball to HIS right . . .

Meek shoots and, too late, the Celtic 'keeper realises he is going the wrong way . . .

GOAL! The ball flies past Thomson's LEFT side for Rangers' opening goal.

GOAL 2 Thirteen minutes later — McPhail gets goal No. 2.

GOAL 3 Two minutes later—Archibald shoots from the wing and scores.

GOAL 4 80 minutes gone — and Archibald nets the last goal.

ON OTHER PAGES

PAGE 2: Malcolm Munro, Bobby Maitland, Ian Peebles; Memory Man; Place the Ball; Letters.

PAGE 3: Davy Wilson (Rangers); Billy McNeill (Celtic); Juniors by Tommy Workman; Racing.

PAGES 4 AND 5: Thrilling, panoramic Hampden scene with today's personality players; memories of the 1928 "giants;" Fitba' Daph cartoons; facts about the final.

PAGE 7: Flashback in pictures to Cup dramas of the past; your pre-match entertainment programme; history of the Cup.

PAGE 8: Big pictures of Celtic and Rangers.

. . . And don't miss tonight's GREEN — big-game reports plus full page of action pictures

TOM FINNEY

PRESTON AND ENGLAND

Best Wishes
Tom Finney

P. TREVILLION /57

A 1957 original, signed by Tom Finney, which was published as
part of the Soccer Sketchbook series.

MUD-LARKS

TOTTENHAM 6. LEICESTER 0.

THE RAIN TRIED ITS HARDEST TO MAKE THIS MATCH A **WASH-OUT**

PROGRAMME

IN FACT TOTTENHAM ENJOYED THE CONDITIONS AND FINISHED WITH A **FLOOD** OF 6 GOALS

BUT NOTHING COULD **DAMPEN** THE EFFERVESCENT PLAY OF SKIPPER (1 GOAL) **BLANCHFLOWER** NOR THE MANNER IN WHICH MEDWIN **SLOSHED** IN 4 NET BUSTERS

SENDING LEICESTER **SLIDING** NEARER TO DIVISION **2**

Help!

AND HELPING TO **WASH AWAY** THEIR OWN RELEGATION **BLUES**

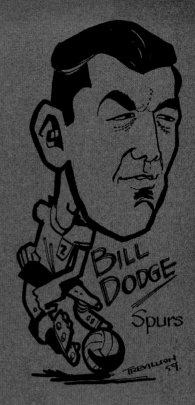

BILL DODGE

Spurs

TREVILLION 59.

HAPPY - NEW - YEAR

Snuff out those cigars
And finish your chicken,
And give your opponents
A jolly good licking.
You can serve better football
Than you have in the past,
It's so bad you must know
It can't possibly last.
The defence has been weak,
And the passing's been poor
And there's times when it seems
That you never will score.
Yet for all this we know
You can put our place right
And show that the cockerel
Has plenty of fight.
And should you get a visit
From Old Mother Luck,
We'll cheer you at Wembley
When you've got the Cup.

'ERE Y'ARE SPURS! A NEW YEARS RESOLUTION WIV' A DIF'RENCE!

EXIT

TREVILLION

Neat Mover

ENGLAND outside-right Bryan Douglas lost his international place during the World Cup. But many critics believe he will hold on to it once he gets a second chance.

The big question is—can Blackburn hold on to Douglas? Some big offers are being made for him.

Bryan **DOUGLAS** (Blackburn)

PTREVILLION 58

Bobby Charlton
Manchester United

Now coming back to his best after a somewhat lean spell, Manchester United inside-forward **BOBBY CHARLTON** has experience to go with his ability and should hold a permanent place in the England line-up.

The Bobby

BOBBY CHARLTON HAS CRAMMED MORE THRILLS, SPILLS AND EXCITEMENT INTO HIS 26 YEARS THAN MOST PEOPLE EXPERIENCE IN A LIFETIME. BOBBY CHARLTON HAS KNOWN TRAGEDY, TOO...

MUNICH, FEB 6TH, 1958. OUT OF THE TWISTED WRECKAGE OF A B.E.A. ELIZABETHAN AIRCRAFT STAGGERED A FAIR-HAIRED 20 YEAR-OLD-BOY... HIS SOCCER APPRENTICESHIP ABRUPTLY ENDED BY THE SUDDEN NEED TO BECOME A MAN

CHARLTON, ONCE THE INFANT OF THE "BABES", GREW UP OVERNIGHT AND ON HIS YOUNG SHOULDERS WEIGHED MUCH OF THE RESPONSIBILITY OF RE-ESTABLISHING MANCHESTER UNITED AS A WORLD FORCE

The Bobby Charlton Story

How it began

BOBBY CHARLTON, WHOSE SOCCER GENIUS HAS GRACED THE MIGHTIEST STADIUMS IN THE WORLD, TODAY RECALLS HIS SCHOOLDAYS AT BEDLINGTON GRAMMAR SCHOOL, ASHINGTON...

"YOU REMEMBER THE PITCHES! THEY WERE PRETTY BAD."

.. HOME GAMES WERE ON THE MINERS' WELFARE GROUNDS

"..THEN THE TRAVELLING TO AWAY MATCHES. ALWAYS WENT BY CORPORATION 'BUS"

LOOK OUT, BLYTHE GRAMMAR HERE WE COME!

I REMEMBER ONCE WE GOT A MEAL AFTER THE GAME. I THOUGHT, 'THIS IS LAVISH' ...BUT IT NEVER HAPPENED AGAIN.

2

Charlton Story

CHARLTON DID HIS TASK MANFULLY AND BECAME KNOWN AS "BOBBY DAZZLER." THE BOY WITH THE SHOT! OF HIS SHOOTING POWER, CHARLTON SAYS...

THE CHANCE COMES... YOU SEE IT... AND YOU HIT IT!

A MODEST EXPLANATION FROM THE BOY WHO, IN OCTOBER 1963, BECAME ENGLAND'S TOP INTERNATIONAL GOALSCORER WITH 31 IN 46 GAMES

IN SEPTEMBER, ENGLAND'S CAPTAIN, JIMMY ARMFIELD, HAD THIS TO SAY...

BOBBY WOULD ALWAYS BE IN MY TEAM. AGAINST SWITZERLAND, HE WENT PAST HIS OPPONENT AS THOUGH NO ONE WAS THERE

IN SEVEN YEARS OF TOP CLASS FOOTBALL, BOBBY CHARLTON HAS BECOME THE MAN THEY ALL LOVE TO TALK ABOUT...

I'M PLEASED TO SAY HE'S THE SAME BOY WHO SIGNED ON AT 15. THAT'S THE FINEST COMPLIMENT I CAN PAY ANYONE

Denis Law

HE'S THE BEST OUTSIDE-LEFT I'VE EVER PARTNERED

Matt Busby

Walter Winterbottom

I COULD TALK FOR EVER ABOUT BOBBY CHARLTON. HE HAS THE GREATEST POTENTIAL AND CAN BECOME ONE OF THE GREATEST PLAYERS EVER!

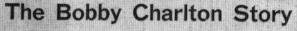

The Bobby Charlton Story

BOBBY CHARLTON HASN'T ALWAYS BEEN A MANCHESTER UNITED FAN...

AS A LAD, I USED TO SUPPORT NEWCASTLE. IT WAS THE ONLY TEAM I COULD AFFORD TO SEE!

HE ADDS, "IF I'D TWO AND A PENNY, I WAS ABLE TO WORK IT IN. THAT GOT ME INTO THE GROUND, MY BUS FARE AND A HOT PIE."

AND THE HERO OF ST. JAMES' PARK AT THE TIME... "WOR JACKIE" MILBURN... BOBBY'S SECOND COUSIN!

TODAY, NEWCASTLE DIRECTOR MR. STAN SEYMOUR REFLECTS ON WHAT MIGHT HAVE BEEN...

I ALWAYS HAD THE FEELING BOBBY WOULD MAKE A CHAMPION. ON THE VERY DAY I HAD AN APPOINTMENT TO MEET HIM, I GOT A MESSAGE, "HE'S GONE TO SEE MATT BUSBY." I KNEW THEN, THAT THAT WAS THAT!

Soccer Sketchbook—6

Johnny HAYNES
FULHAM AND ENGLAND

● Quick-thinking left-back Tommy Tanks saved his side from conceding many a goal with his sudden decisions.

● In the match against City there were only a few minutes left for play when Tanks spotted the unmarked opposing centre-forward. Quick as a flash, Tommy realised it was only his presence that played the forward on-side. That's when Tommy raced off the field appealing for off-side.

● The centre-forward collected the ball and raced on to score. Was it a goal?

WHAT'S COOKING

EASTER HAVING BEEN AND GONE TOTTENHAM CAN NOW FORGET ABOUT **CRACKING** EASTER EGGS AND CONCENTRATE ON **CRACKING** THE LUTON DEFENCE

what a lucky break

BUT THIS WON'T BE EASY FOR LUTON ARE NO **SLOWCOACHES** AS SHOWN BY THEIR AMAZING CUP **RUN**

AND LET'S REMEMBER THEY GOBBLED UP THE NORWICH CANARY AND OBVIOUSLY INTEND DOING THE SAME TO THE SPURS **COCKEREL**

BUT WITH LUTON HAVING TO KEEP ONE EYE ON WEMBLEY I CAN'T SEE THIS HAPPENING

I FANCY IF ANYBODY'S GOOSE IS GOING TO BE COOKED IT WILL BE **LUTON'S**

4 April 1959. Tottenham won 3-0. Luton went on to lose that season's FA Cup final 2-1 to Nottingham Forest.

Reg MATTHEWS
Chelsea

HEY, REF!

MUST be a goal. F.A. Law 12 states that no player may leave the field of play or return without receiving a signal from the referee.

Tiger, 13 April 1963 – one of many Roy of the Rovers strips drawn by Trevillion in the early 1960s.

IF YOU WERE THE REF

1. A forward takes a shot at an open goal, but just as the ball is about to enter the net, a spectator rushes on to the field and kicks the ball clear. Would you allow a goal?

2. Two players blame each other for the mistakes which have resulted in goals and come to blows in their own penalty area. What decision must you make?

3. A player takes a throw-in and throws the ball back to his own goalkeeper, who completely misses the ball. Would you allow a goal?

4. A player taking an indirect free kick inside the penalty area hits the upright. But the ball rebounds to him and he cracks it into the net. Is it a goal? You're the ref!

5. A forward is running to take a pass when a defender stands in front of him, waving his arms, preventing him getting to the ball. Would you blow your whistle?

6. You award a goal, then a linesman calls your attention to something that happened *before* the goal was scored. You realise you have made a mistake, but can you reverse your previous decision?

7. The goalie takes a goal-kick by tapping the ball a few yards into the penalty area. His full-back, standing just inside the penalty area, passes back to the goalie so that he can pick up the ball and fly-kick downfield. Is there anything wrong with this?

8. Before the start of a match, you have had cause to order a player off the field for misconduct. Would you allow another man to take the place of the player ordered off?

9. From a throw-in the ball strikes you and bounces back to the thrower, who promptly kicks it into midfield. Would you blow your whistle and stop the game—and why?

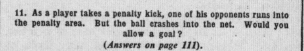

10. A winger is about to take a corner kick when you signal "half time". But should you have allowed the kick to be taken before stopping play?

11. As a player takes a penalty kick, one of his opponents runs into the penalty area. But the ball crashes into the net. Would you allow a goal?
(Answers on page 111).

75

If You Were The Ref, Roy of the Rovers Annual 1965.

RIGHT OR WRONG ?
Answers to If You Were the Ref

1. No. Law 10 makes it quite clear that a goal cannot be allowed unless the ball crosses the goal-line. In this case you would "order off" the spectator and then award a dropped ball on the spot where the interference took place.

2. Law 12 states you shall deal with them by caution or dismissal from play, and if the game has been stopped to administer either caution or dismissal, the game shall be restarted by an indirect free-kick against the offending team.

3. No goal! Law 15 which concerns throw-in's states that in this sort of situation a corner kick shall be awarded to the other team.

4. No. In the case of all free kicks, the player shall not play the ball a second time until it has been kicked by another player. In this case you would give an indirect kick to the other side.

5. Most definitely! This is deliberate obstruction. You would caution the player and then award the other side an indirect free-kick.

6. The linesman is quite right to call the ref's attention to any infringement and if the game has not restarted after a goal has been signalled, that goal can be cancelled. But once the ball has been kicked off again following the award of a goal, the ref cannot reverse his decision. (Law 5.)

7. Yes. The Law concerning goal-kicks states that the ball must be kicked direct into play, beyond the penalty area, before it can be returned to the goalie for a fly-kick. In this case the ball did NOT go outside the penalty area, so you would order the kick to be retaken.

8. Yes. You have full control the moment you step on to the pitch, so you have the power to send off a player even before the kick-off. If this happened, however, you would allow a substitute to take the field.

9. The man taking a throw-in is not allowed to play the ball a second time until it has been touched by another player—and in this case you are NOT a player. Indirect free-kick for the other side.

10. You were quite right. The moment 45 minutes have been played, you must call a halt. The only reason for allowing the play to continue is for the taking of a penalty kick—but not for a corner.

11. It's a goal and no doubt about it. Although every other player except the kicker must remain outside the area when a penalty is being taken, Law 14 makes it quite clear that if a defender enters the area as the ball is being kicked you would not intervene until the penalty had been taken. If the ball entered the net you would allow the goal. If the kick was missed or saved by the goalie, you would order it to be retaken.

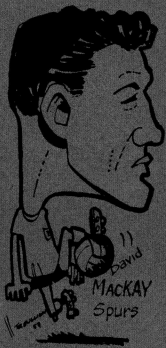

David MACKAY Spurs

HEY, REF!

★ Tom Linney is famed for his heading ability and the crowd are yelling "goal" as he goes for this high centre. It looks out of reach, but the incredible Tom makes it by leaning on the shoulders of a team-mate. A great performance. No wonder the crowd roars as the ball crashes in the back of the net.

The beaten goalkeeper appeals to the referee. What's the verdict?

Answer at foot of Column 3.

MEL HOPKINS (Spurs)

Watch Perry

BLACKPOOL'S South African - born outside-left Bill Perry goes on the short list for the wing position in the England team.

A former England international, Perry, a fast and direct player, lost his place in rather surprising circumstances.

On two occasions already this season, England team manager Walter Winterbottom has seen Perry star for Blackpool.

BILL PERRY (Blackpool)

DID YOU KNOW
SERIES OF 50: CARD NO. 34

1933

EVERTON WON DIVISION 2, DIVISION I CHAMPIONSHIPS AND CUP IN 3 SUCCESSIVE SEASONS

Cardmaster Football Tips

SERIES OF 50.   CARD No. 11

Long Kicking

For long kicks you must use the instep and point your toe towards the ground. Bend the knee well over the ball and, as the kick is made, straighten it out and let the foot follow straight through until the leg is almost horizontal. For an instep kick with a dead or placed ball repeat the above but have the ball about level with the toe of the other foot at the moment of kicking.

Hey, Ref!

● No goal. F.A. Law 12 states the referee must award an indirect free kick to the opposing side and caution the player for ungentlemanly conduct.

JIMMY GREAVES STORY
by TREVILLION

ON FEBRUARY 20th 1940, THE GREATEST GOAL SCORER IN MODERN FOOTBALL WAS BORN. HE WAS CHRISTENED –

JAMES PETER GREAVES.

ALMOST AS SOON AS HE COULD WALK, JIMMY WAS KICKING A BALL AROUND, BUT HE WAS A SMALL LAD FOR HIS AGE SO HIS SCHOOL FRIENDS PUT HIM IN GOAL.

CHELSEA SCOUT, JIMMY (BOWLER-HAT) THOMPSON, ARRANGED FOR GREAVES TO JOIN CHELSEA. THE DATE – OCTOBER 16th, 1955.

SEASON 1957/58 SAW 17-YEAR-OLD GREAVES MAKE HIS FIRST DIVISION DEBUT AGAINST SPURS AT TOTTENHAM.

ALTHOUGH OPPOSED BY IRISH INTERNATIONAL DANNY BLANCHFLOWER, THE DYNAMIC GREAVES SCORED THE GOAL THAT GAVE HIS SIDE A 1-1 DRAW.

NOW ESTABLISHED IN THE CHELSEA FIRST TEAM, JIMMY OPENED THE 1958 SEASON WITH FIVE GOALS IN CHELSEA'S 6-2 DEFEAT OF THE NEW CHAMPIONS WOLVES. SAID WOLVES MANAGER, STAN CULLIS, AT THE TIME.....

WHAT A PLAYER! THEY SAY HE DOESN'T RUN AROUND ENOUGH. HE WOULDN'T HAVE TO FOR ME. I'D TELL HIM TO STAND AROUND AND WAIT. THAT WOULD BE ENOUGH.

1959 AND 19-YEAR-OLD GREAVES IS PICKED FOR ENGLAND. HE SCORES A GREAT GOAL BUT PERU WIN 4-1.

BY MAY 1961 AND IN JUST FOUR SEASONS (157 GAMES) GREAVES HAD SCORED 129 GOALS – THE FASTEST CENTURY ON RECORD.

JIMMY IS SOON BANGING THEM IN FOR TOTTENHAM. HE FINISHES THE SEASON TOP SCORER WITH 29 GOALS, ONE OF THEM BEING IN SPURS 3-1 VICTORY OVER BURNLEY IN THE CUP FINAL AT WEMBLEY.

BEFORE THE FINAL GREAVES HAD PREDICTED HE WOULD SCORE IN THE FIRST FIVE MINUTES..... HE DID JUST THAT.

1963 AND THANKS TO TWO GOALS FROM GREAVES SPURS BEAT ATHLETICO MADRID 5-1 TO WIN THE EUROPEAN CUP WINNER'S CUP.

GOALS, GOALS, GOALS AND STILL MORE GOALS FOR GREAVES, BUT NOVEMBER 1965 SEES THE FLOW ABRUPTLY STOPPED. JAUNDICE PUTS HIM OUT OF FOOTBALL FOR THIRTEEN WEEKS, WHEN HE RETURNS HE IS BUT A SHADOW OF HIS GLORIOUS BEST.

WAKE UP, GREAVES

HE FAILS TO FIND A PLACE IN ENGLAND'S 1966 WORLD CUP WINNING TEAM AND MANY THINK HIS ENGLAND AND SPURS CAREER IS COMING TO AN END.

SO IT WAS NO SURPRISE WHEN HE GAVE UP STOPPING GOALS TO SCORING THEM – AND NOT ONLY IN ONE'S AND TWO'S. HE SOMETIMES MANAGED A DOZEN AT A TIME.

THIS DIDN'T PLEASE JIM, FOR EVEN IN THOSE DAYS HE FANCIED HIMSELF AS A FORWARD – HIS IDOL BEING THE ENGLAND AND NEWCASTLE INSIDE FORWARD – LEN SHACKLETON.

HIS MAIN JOB AT CHELSEA.....

TELEPHONE EXCHANGE OPERATOR.

FROM THE TELEPHONE LINE TO THE FORWARD LINE. GREAVES SCORED 154 GOALS IN TWO SEASONS FOR THE CHELSEA COLTS.

JUNE 1961 AND A BOMBSHELL FOR CHELSEA FANS. GOALSCORER EXTRAORDINARY, GREAVES JOINS AC MILAN FOR £83,000.

HIS SORTIE INTO ITALIAN FOOTBALL WAS A BRIEF ONE. HE SPENT ONLY ONE-THIRD OF THE SEASON WITH AC MILAN AND WAS NEVER HAPPY THERE. YET AT THE END OF THE ITALIAN SEASON GREAVES IS AC'S SECOND HIGHEST GOAL SCORER.

ON HIS RETURN TO ENGLAND SPURS PAID £1 UNDER £100,000 FOR HIS SERVICES. SAID TOTTENHAM'S MANAGER BILLY NICHOLSON.....

I DIDN'T WANT GREAVES TO BE BURDENED WITH A £100,000 PRICE TAG.

CHELSEA MUST BE CRAZY SELLING HIM. HE'S THE ONLY ONE WHO KEEPS THEM IN THE FIRST DIVISION.

THE FANS WERE RIGHT, THE FOLLOWING SEASON CHELSEA WERE RELEGATED.

SECOND DIVISION CLUBS – MIDDLESBROUGH AND BIRMINGHAM MAKE BIDS FOR HIM BUT TOTTENHAM TURNED THEM DOWN. SEASON 1968/69 LOOMS UP AS THE BIG TEST FOR GREAVES.

GOOD OLD JIMMY!

JIMMY IS EQUAL TO THE CHALLENGE. IN FACT, SO MUCH SO, THAT HIS GOAL SCORING FEATS HAVE THE FANS CHANTING FOR RAMSEY TO RECALL HIM TO THE ENGLAND TEAM.

TODAY GREAVES IS AS PHYSICALLY AND MENTALLY FIT AS HE HAS EVER BEEN AND THE SIGNS ARE THAT THERE ARE MANY MORE MOMENTS OF GLORY HEADING HIS WAY.

WHAT IS GREAVES' GOAL SCORING SECRET? WELL WHO BETTER TO GO TO FOR THE ANSWER THAN GREAVES HIMSELF?

IN MY JOB YOU HAVE JUST ONE SECOND IN WHICH TO MAKE EVERY DECISION. JUST IMAGINE YOU, YOURSELF, TRYING TO DO THAT IN YOUR JOB. BUT THAT'S WHAT IT'S LIKE IN FRONT OF GOAL. SO I LET MY LEGS DO JUST WHAT THEY WANT AND TRUST THEY DO THE RIGHT THING.

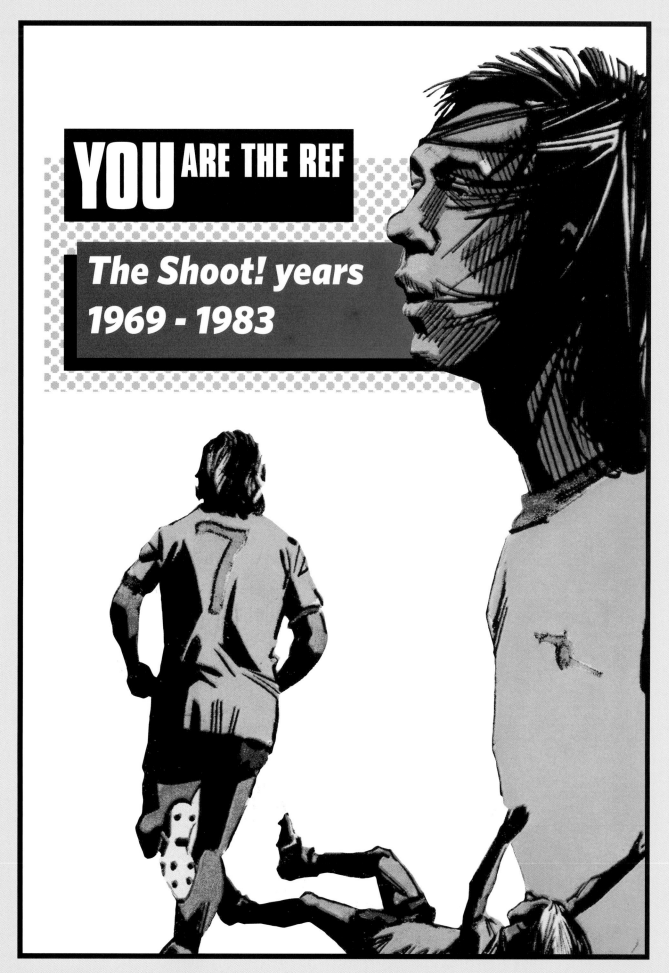

YOU ARE THE REF

The Shoot! years
1969 - 1983

We've spotted the dodgers

WHO are the football dodgers? How do they work their tricks? Trevillion, the brilliant sports artist, has been finding out. And today he kicks off the season with a revealing series every fan — and referee — will want to study. Trevillion will look at the dodgers again next week. Watch for him.

"£200 a week they pay him and he can't take a throw-in —wants bloody shooting. . . ." The crowd really have a go at a player when he's pulled up for a foul throw, but what they don't realise is that more than half the throw-ins taken in a match are illegal. Players are getting away with it because too many officials are falling down on the job.

—RON SUART, Chelsea's assistant manager.

DAVID WEBB

Webb, Bremner, Smith and players like these are textbook throwers, but they're a dying breed. I'll show you why.

A player must have some part of both feet on the ground when he throws. The Continentals showed us the way round this law — a throw-in on the "walk." With one foot off the ground a player gets a lot of extra beef into the throw.

TOMMY SMITH

The long throw is a specialised art or it was until last season when practically every team produced a lad capable of hurling one inside the box. How? Because the ball was released in FRONT of the forehead, and that's illegal. The ball must be released OVER the head.

LEGAL

FOUL

BALL THROWN HERE

The more the arms straighten, the more leverage

The thrower must face the field — or so the law states. The quick-throw experts made nonsense of this with a quick pick-up and a throw down the line. Nobody cared which way the thrower's body faced.

If a straight line drawn in front of the thrower does not cross the touchline, the throw's illegal.

Fans call it quick thinking when a player throws the ball against an opponent and collects the rebound. It's not — it's ungentlemanly conduct, a foul throw.

YOU ARE THE REF

● Compiled by STAN LOVER, Chairman of the London Referees' Society

1 At a corner-kick a goalkeeper stands in front of an attacker and by using his arms, prevents the opponent from reaching the ball. What is your decision?

2 After 30 minutes of your match, play is held up for two minutes for treatment to an injured player. Do you add the two minutes to the end of the first-half or the second?

3 A goalkeeper appears in a black jersey for a Football League match. Is this in order?

4 You've ordered a penalty-kick to be retaken. The player who took the first kick refuses to take it again. His captain calls another player. Do you object?

5

A A player, in his own penalty-area, strikes a spectator. At the time the ball is outside the penalty-area, but after stopping play and sending off the player you award a penalty-kick.

B From the penalty-kick the ball is played back to a team-mate who runs into the penalty-area and scores. You decide to disallow the goal and order the penalty to be retaken.

C The goalkeeper moves from his goal-line before the ball is kicked into the goal. You decide to award a goal. (Where is the problem?)

ANSWERS

1. You should award a penalty-kick for holding an opponent.

2. Two minutes should be added to the time elapsed during the first-half.

3. No. The official colours for goalkeepers in Football League matches are scarlet, royal blue, green or white.

4. No.

5. The problem is in A. The penalty-kick decision is incorrect because the offence was not committed against an opponent and is defined as Violent Conduct. The correct award is an indirect free-kick where the offence occured.
In B the decision is correct because the ball was not kicked forward.
In C the action of the 'keeper, in moving before the ball is kicked, is ignored if the ball goes into the goal!

16 DECEMBER 1972

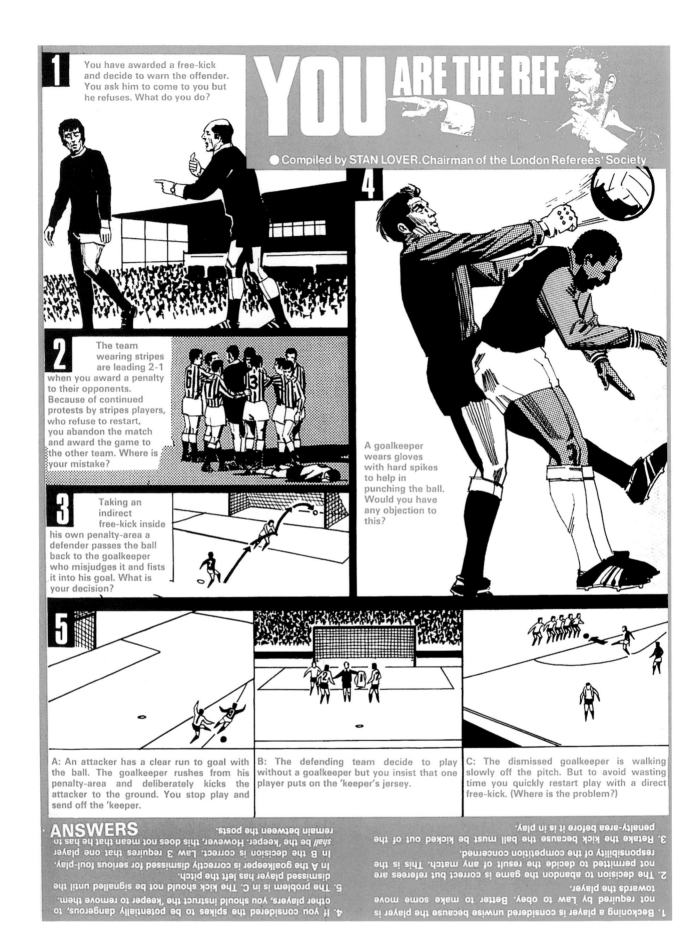

YOU ARE THE REF

● Compiled by STAN LOVER. Chairman of the London Referees' Society

1 You have awarded a free-kick and decide to warn the offender. You ask him to come to you but he refuses. What do you do?

2 The team wearing stripes are leading 2-1 when you award a penalty to their opponents. Because of continued protests by stripes players, who refuse to restart, you abandon the match and award the game to the other team. Where is your mistake?

3 Taking an indirect free-kick inside his own penalty-area a defender passes the ball back to the goalkeeper who misjudges it and fists it into his goal. What is your decision?

4 A goalkeeper wears gloves with hard spikes to help in punching the ball. Would you have any objection to this?

5

A: An attacker has a clear run to goal with the ball. The goalkeeper rushes from his penalty-area and deliberately kicks the attacker to the ground. You stop play and send off the 'keeper.

B: The defending team decide to play without a goalkeeper but you insist that one player puts on the 'keeper's jersey.

C: The dismissed goalkeeper is walking slowly off the pitch. But to avoid wasting time you quickly restart play with a direct free-kick. (Where is the problem?)

ANSWERS

1. Beckoning a player is considered unwise because the player is not required by Law to obey. Better to make some move towards the player.

2. The decision to abandon the game is correct but referees are not permitted to decide the result of any match. This is the responsibility of the competition concerned.

3. Retake the kick because the ball must be kicked out of the penalty-area before it is in play.

4. If you considered the spikes to be potentially dangerous, to other players, you should instruct the 'keeper to remove them.

5. The problem is in C. The kick should not be signalled until the dismissed player has left the pitch.
In A the goalkeeper is correctly dismissed for serious foul-play.
In B the decision is correct. Law 3 requires that one player *shall* be the 'keeper. However, this does not mean that he has to remain between the posts.

17 MARCH 1973

YOU ARE THE REF

Compiled by STAN LOVER, Chairman of the London Referees' Society

1 During the game you — the referee — twist an ankle. You stop play and receive attention. How should play be restarted?

2 An attacker leans on the shoulders of an opponent to gain height in order to head the ball. Is this an offence?

3 During your match you see two players from the same team about to change shirts. Do you take any action?

4 During a floodlit match a Press photographer takes pictures by flashlight. Is this allowed?

5

A: Two opposing players kick the ball at exactly the same moment and it goes over the goal-line. You decide to drop the ball to restart play.

B: When you drop the ball it falls to an attacker who is in an offside position. You stop play and award a free-kick to the defending team.

C: From the free-kick the ball is kicked into the opposite goal. You award a goal-kick. (Where is the problem?)

ANSWERS

1. Restart by dropping the ball where it was when play was stopped.

2. Yes. The attacker must be penalised for holding an opponent.

3. No.

4. No, because flashlights could distract the players.

5. The problem is in B. A player cannot be offside from a dropped ball.
In A the action taken is fair and avoids either team gaining an unfair advantage.
In C the decision is correct because the award for an offside offence is an *indirect* free-kick.

14 APRIL 1973

1872
The road to The Oval in 1871-72—the first season of the FA Cup—is peppered with clubs like Harrow Chequers, Donington School (Spalding), Hampstead Heathens and the Civil Service.
In these days the Kennington Oval is the mecca of soccer. (They even play the semi-finals there until 1882). In the first year entries for the FA Cup reach 15. Two clubs scratch—the eventual finalists Royal Engineers and Wanderers subsequently receiving walk-overs—and three are given byes. Queen's Park, Glasgow, in fact, reach the semi-final without kicking a ball. They are given a bye in the first round, a walk-over in the second and a bye in the third. Having drawn with Wanderers in the semi-final, they decide that travelling again from Glasgow to The Oval for the replay will wreck the club's finances—so they scratch.
The first final, refereed by A. Stair, of Upton Park, attracts nearly 2000 to The Oval. Wanderers beat Royal Engineers 1—0.

1887
The FA Cup Final is played at The Oval. Bayliss (West Bromwich Albion) heads for goal but Warner (Aston Villa) saves. Villa won 2—0.

£10 REWARD,
STOLEN!
ENGLISH CUP

1895
The Cup was never found.

1914
The first Royal Cup Final. The rival captains, Boyle (Burnley) and Ferguson (Liverpool), leave the Royal Box having been presented to King George V before the match. Burnley won 1—0.

1930
A quickly-taken free-kick by James before half-time sets Arsenal on the road to victory; James to Bastin, a perfect return pass, and James shot into the Huddersfield net.

1932
Newcastle beat Arsenal with the most disputed goal of the age. Photographs confirm that the ball was out of play before Richardson hooks it back for Allen to head home.

1933
The immortal Dixie Dean bundles himself and the ball into the net in Everton's 3—1 conquest of Manchester City.

ALEX JAMES

DIXIE DEAN

1946
Bert Turner (Charlton) puts the ball into his own net, and Derby go on to gain a sensational 4—1 victory.

1961
Tottenham become the first team to win the Double since Aston Villa in 1897. Banks of Leicester tries in vain to stop Tottenham's second goal. Tottenham Hotspur 2, Leicester City 0.

1953
The Stanley Matthews Cup Final. The immortal Blackpool right-winger stars in the sensational 4—3 victory over Bolton Wanderers.

OMENTS

Devised and drawn by Trevillion

1923
First Wembley Final and the stadium is invaded by a multitude estimated at 250,000. The tidal wave is eased back with the help of a policeman on a white horse.

1927
Lewis, the Arsenal goalkeeper, allows the ball to slip out of his hands and trickle over his goal-line. A tragic error which allows Cardiff to take the Cup out of England for the first time.

DAN LEWIS

1937
The first Final to be screened on television and Sunderland's first success in the Cup. Carter scores the second goal in Sunderland's 3—1 win over Preston North End.

1938
Mutch scores for Preston from the penalty-spot against Huddersfield in the last minute of extra time.

RAICH CARTER

CHARLIE GEORGE

1970
Defender David Webb (Chelsea) scores the winning goal in extra time in the FA Cup replay against Leeds.

1971
Flat on his back, Charlie George (Arsenal) acknowledges the cheers of the crowd. Arsenal have beaten Liverpool 2—1 and have matched Tottenham's Double-winning exploit of 10 years ago.

1972
HOW THEY HAVE REACHED WEMBLEY . . .
ARSENAL.—Third round: Swindon 0, Arsenal 2 (Armstrong, Ball). Fourth round: Reading 1, Arsenal 2 (Morgan o.g., Rice). Fifth round: Derby 2, Arsenal 2 (George 2). Fifth round replay: Arsenal 0, Derby 0, after extra time. Fifth round second replay: Derby 0, Arsenal 1 (Kennedy), at Leicester. Sixth round: Orient 0, Arsenal 1 (Ball). Semi-final: Arsenal 1 (Armstrong), Stoke 1, at Villa Park. Semi-final replay: Arsenal 2 (George pen., Radford), Stoke 1, at Goodison Park.

LEEDS UNITED.—Third round: Leeds 4 (Giles 2, 1 pen., Lorimer 2), Bristol Rovers 1. Fourth round: Liverpool 0, Leeds 0. Fourth round replay: Leeds 2 (Clarke 2), Liverpool 0. Fifth round: Cardiff 0, Leeds 2 (Giles 2). Sixth round: Leeds 2 (Clarke, Charlton), Tottenham 1. Semi-final: Leeds 3 (Jones 2, Lorimer), Birmingham 0, at Hillsborough.

THE FINAL
ARSENAL .... LEEDS UNITED ....

YOU ARE THE REF

Compiled by STAN LOVER, Chairman of the London Referees' Society

1 You have instructed a player not to take a direct free-kick until you signal. But when you are moving back defenders the kick is taken and the ball goes into goal. Do you (a) allow the goal, (b) disallow the goal and award a free-kick to the opposing team or (c) caution the kicker and have the kick retaken?

2 Is the minimum height of the corner flagpost (a) 5 ft., (b) 5 ft. 6 ins. or (c) 6 ft.?

3 At a penalty-kick, the penalty-taker steps over the ball and allows a team-mate to run in and score from the spot. Do you (a) allow the goal, (b) penalise the first penalty-taker for offside, or (c) have the penalty retaken?

4 A defender uses the shoulders of a team-mate to gain height before heading the ball. Do you (a) take no action, (b) caution the player and award a direct free-kick, or (c) caution him and award an indirect free-kick?

A: From a long throw-in the ball goes directly to a player standing in an offside position.

B: The ball is then kicked past another attacker (white shirt) standing, next to the goalkeeper and a second opponent, on the goal-line. A goal is awarded.

C: At the kick-off only one player of the team kicking-off is in the 10 yard circle when you blow your whistle to start. (Where is the problem?)

ANSWERS

1. The kicker should be cautioned (c) and the kick retaken. 2. The minimum height is 5 ft. (a). 3. The penalty-kick should be retaken (c) because of encroachment by the second player before the ball was kicked. 4. The defender should be cautioned and an indirect free-kick awarded (c). 5. The problem is in B. The attacker is offside not having at least two opponents between himself and the goal-line. In A a player is not offside if he receives the ball direct from a throw-in. In C the Laws do not require a minimum number of players to be inside the 10 yard circle at a kick-off.

1 SEPTEMBER 1973

YOU ARE THE REF

Compiled by STAN LOVER, Chairman of the London Referees' Society

1 An attacker, whose team is leading, takes the ball to his opponents' corner and shields it. An opponent runs off the pitch, around the attacker and kicks the ball upfield. Would you (a) take no action, (b) award a free-kick against the attacker for time wasting or (c) caution the opponent for leaving the pitch?

2 Is the maximum width of a pitch (a) 90 metres, (b) 100 metres or (c) 110 metres?

3 Time expires as a penalty is about to be taken. The 'keeper moves off his line before the ball is kicked but the ball goes over the crossbar. Would you (a) blow for full-time, (b) caution the 'keeper after ending the match or (c) order the penalty to be re-taken?

4 At half-time a team captain enters your dressing-room and uses foul language against you. Would you (a) report him to his Team Manager, (b) refuse to allow him to play in the second-half or (c) insist that a substitute replaces him?

5 A: Running forward with the ball an attacker passes a team-mate who is in an off-side position. You take no action.

B: The ball is then played back to the second attacker who shoots goalwards past the first attacker. You blow your whistle for offside.

C: Before the whistle was blown the ball had entered the goal and was out of play. You decide to award a goal-kick. (Where is the problem?)

ANSWERS

1. Take no action (a). The attacker is not shielding the ball illegally and the opponent leaves the pitch in order to play the ball. 2. Maximum width is 90 metres (a). 3. Another penalty must be taken (c). 4. Refuse to allow the player to take any further part in the match (b). 5. The problem is in C. A free-kick should be awarded for the offside offence and not a goal-kick. In A there is no offside offence if the first attacker retains possession of the ball. In B the offside decision is correct because the second attacker is not in an offside position and is not interfering with play.

22 SEPTEMBER 1973

Penalty? Give him an Oscar

"On average, 60 per cent. of penalty kicks are 'bought' by play-acting. Usually the more skilful the ball player, the better the actor — although I'm convinced that George Best, for all his faults, has never ONCE been guilty of 'buying' a foul."

—PAT JENNINGS, Spurs.

The skilful dribbler is best able to fake a foul because he can take the ball past an opponent LATE, CLOSE and QUICK. But maybe, having tricked his opponent, he finds he has overplayed his hand.

For instance, if he knocks the ball too far forward, it's out of play.

If he allows a defender on his blind side to intercept, he loses the ball.

If he fails to spot the goalkeeper is racing out to swoop on the ball, he's had it.

So he can now attempt to "buy" a foul and win a penalty.

There are three ways he can do this:

He allows his back foot to drag so making contact with his opponent, tripping himself.

An attempted hurdle over the defender's outstretched leg . . . contact! A spectacular fall.

He dummies his opponent into going right then deliberately runs into him, making it appear he's been body-checked.

Play-acting off the ball also wins penalties. A closely marked forward, waiting for a centre, will dart forward a yard—stop—dart forward—stop—then, as the centre's hit, FEINT to go again, causing the defender to run into his back. A spectacular forward tumble helps make it look a blatant push from behind.

STOP — GO — STOP — GO — FEINT

The cheekiest penalty I've seen won was by a forward who, having noticed three Spurs defenders had their sleeves rolled up, copied them. Ten minutes later, challenging for a ball at waist height, he slipped his arm inside his opponent's and knocked the ball away. Spurs were done for a penalty.

Devised and drawn by PAUL TREVILLION

YOU ARE THE REF

1 When the ball is centred, a defender shouts "my ball" to his goalkeeper who is distracted. No opponents are near. Do you (a) take no action or (b) caution the defender, restarting with a drop-ball?

2 A player with the ball deliberately turns away from an opponent when he is challenged. The opponent charges him in the back. Do you (a) take no action, (b) award an indirect free-kick or (c) a direct free-kick against the opponent?

3 Checking the pitch you notice that no two corner-flags are the same colour. Do you (a) take no action, (b) insist on same coloured flags or (c) take the flags off the posts?

4 You have awarded an indirect free-kick against the defending side, outside the penalty-area. The ball is kicked directly into goal. You disallow it, but the attackers protest that you did not raise an arm to signify an indirect-kick. Do you (a) allow the goal, (b) retake the kick or (c) award a goal-kick?

5

A: The ball is trapped under the body of an injured player when an opponent tries to kick it. You stop play and, after the player is treated, decide to restart by dropping the ball.

B: However, before you drop the ball, two players of each team prepare to play it.

C: After the ball touches the ground a player attempts to kick it, but misses and kicks an opponent. You stop play and award an indirect free-kick.
(Where is the problem?)

ANSWERS

1. Take no action (a). This is a tactical call to a team-mate not intending to distract an opponent. 2. A direct free-kick is the correct award for charging in a dangerous manner (c). A charge from behind, on a shoulder blade, would be allowable but not into an opponent's back. 3. Take no action (a). It is not essential that all corner flags are identical. 4. The kick should be retaken (b) because the arm signal is essential information to the team awarded the kick. 5. The problem is in A. In attempting to kick the ball the opponent is endangering the injured player. The correct decision is an indirect free-kick for dangerous play. In B, there is no problem. No specific number of players must be present at a drop-ball. It is normal to have the same number from each team. In C, the indirect free-kick would be correct for dangerous play because the opponent was not kicked intentionally.

GEORGE BEST STORY

by TREVILLION

ON MAY 22nd 1946, RICHARD BEST, A BELFAST SHIPYARD WORKER, BECAME THE VERY PROUD FATHER OF A BABY BOY. HE WAS CHRISTENED GEORGE. FROM THE MOMENT HE COULD WALK, HIS SOCCER-MAD DAD SAW TO IT THAT THERE WAS A BALL AT HIS FEET.

GEORGE CAME DOWN TO EARTH WITH A BUMP WHEN HE CAME FACE TO FACE WITH THE MANCHESTER UNITED PLAYERS. THEY ALL APPEARED GIANTS TO THE TINY 5'3" 7 STONE LAD FROM BELFAST.

EVERYBODY WAS SITTING UP AND TAKING NOTICE OF THE DARK-HAIRED YOUTH, INCLUDING NORTHERN IRELAND WHO PICKED HIM FOR THEIR GAMES AGAINST WALES AND URUGUAY.

THE FOLLOWING SEASON GEORGE MISSED ONLY ONE FIRST TEAM GAME AND ESTABLISHED HIMSELF AS THE MOST PROMISING STAR IN BRITISH FOOTBALL.

BUT HIS TRIUMPHANT MARCH CAME TO AN END THE NEXT SEASON WHEN HE WAS CUT DOWN BY A SERIOUS KNEE INJURY WHICH NEEDED A CARTILAGE OPERATION. MANY CRITICS CONSIDERED THE LIGHTLY-BUILT YOUNGSTER WITH THE BUILD OF A BALLET DANCER, HAD NOT THE PHYSIQUE FOR THE HARD PHYSICAL WORLD OF FIRST DIVISION FOOTBALL.

STILL THE HONOURS CAME PILING IN AS UNITED WON THE EUROPEAN CUP AND BEST WAS VOTED THE FOOTBALLER OF THE YEAR. ALTHOUGH THE MODEST BEST FELT IN HIS OWN MIND THAT IT SHOULD HAVE GONE TO THE EVERTON AND ENGLAND CENTRE-HALF BRIAN LABONE.

SOCCER-MAD GEORGE, WHO DOES NOT SMOKE AND ADMITS THAT POP SINGER LULU IS HIS FAVOURITE RECORDING STAR, DOES LIKE TO PLAY THE ODD GAME OF SNOOKER OR BILLIARDS. HE ALSO LIKES TO READ COMEDY BOOKS ESPECIALLY BY SPIKE MILLIGAN.

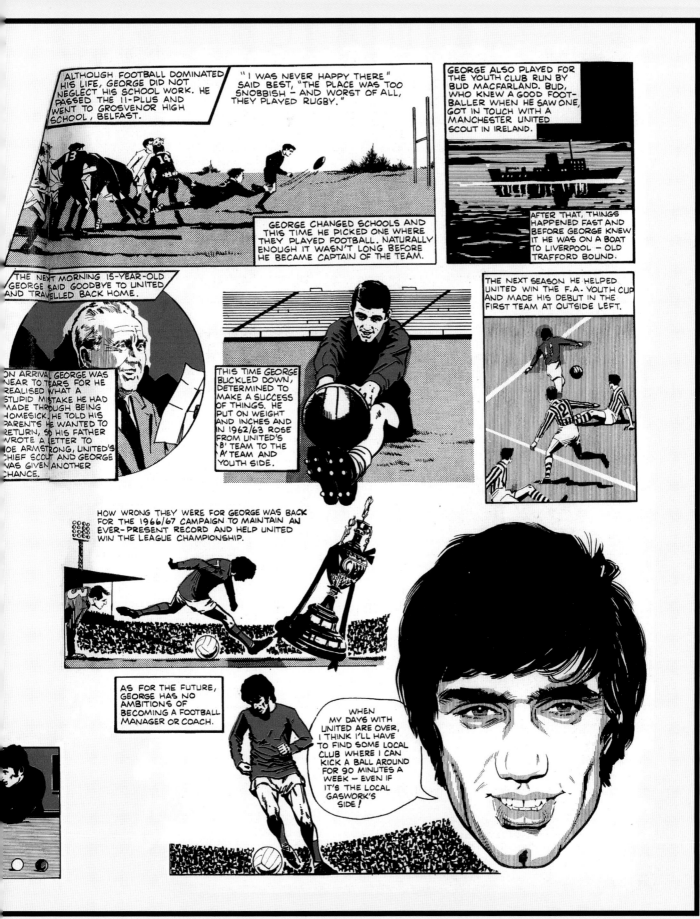

ALTHOUGH FOOTBALL DOMINATED HIS LIFE, GEORGE DID NOT NEGLECT HIS SCHOOL WORK. HE PASSED THE 11-PLUS AND WENT TO GROSVENOR HIGH SCHOOL, BELFAST.

"I WAS NEVER HAPPY THERE" SAID BEST, "THE PLACE WAS TOO SNOBBISH — AND WORST OF ALL, THEY PLAYED RUGBY."

GEORGE ALSO PLAYED FOR THE YOUTH CLUB RUN BY BUD MACFARLAND. BUD, WHO KNEW A GOOD FOOT-BALLER WHEN HE SAW ONE, GOT IN TOUCH WITH A MANCHESTER UNITED SCOUT IN IRELAND.

GEORGE CHANGED SCHOOLS AND THIS TIME HE PICKED ONE WHERE THEY PLAYED FOOTBALL. NATURALLY ENOUGH IT WASN'T LONG BEFORE HE BECAME CAPTAIN OF THE TEAM.

AFTER THAT, THINGS HAPPENED FAST AND BEFORE GEORGE KNEW IT HE WAS ON A BOAT TO LIVERPOOL — OLD TRAFFORD BOUND.

THE NEXT MORNING 15-YEAR-OLD GEORGE SAID GOODBYE TO UNITED AND TRAVELLED BACK HOME.

ON ARRIVAL GEORGE WAS NEAR TO TEARS FOR HE REALISED WHAT A STUPID MISTAKE HE HAD MADE THROUGH BEING HOMESICK. HE TOLD HIS PARENTS HE WANTED TO RETURN, SO HIS FATHER WROTE A LETTER TO JOE ARMSTRONG, UNITED'S CHIEF SCOUT AND GEORGE WAS GIVEN ANOTHER CHANCE.

THIS TIME GEORGE BUCKLED DOWN, DETERMINED TO MAKE A SUCCESS OF THINGS. HE PUT ON WEIGHT AND INCHES AND IN 1962/63 ROSE FROM UNITED'S 'B' TEAM TO THE 'A' TEAM AND YOUTH SIDE.

THE NEXT SEASON HE HELPED UNITED WIN THE F.A. YOUTH CUP AND MADE HIS DEBUT IN THE FIRST TEAM AT OUTSIDE LEFT.

HOW WRONG THEY WERE FOR GEORGE WAS BACK FOR THE 1966/67 CAMPAIGN TO MAINTAIN AN EVER-PRESENT RECORD AND HELP UNITED WIN THE LEAGUE CHAMPIONSHIP.

AS FOR THE FUTURE, GEORGE HAS NO AMBITIONS OF BECOMING A FOOTBALL MANAGER OR COACH.

WHEN MY DAYS WITH UNITED ARE OVER, I THINK I'LL HAVE TO FIND SOME LOCAL CLUB WHERE I CAN KICK A BALL AROUND FOR 90 MINUTES A WEEK — EVEN IF IT'S THE LOCAL GASWORK'S SIDE!

YOU ARE THE REF

1 During a League match the crossbar is cracked and could be dangerous. Do you (a) play on without a crossbar, (b) improvise with a rope or (c) abandon the match?

2 You see a defender intentionally trip an opponent in the penalty-area and award a penalty. However, a neutral linesman says the opponent fell over the defender's leg. Do you (a) insist on a penalty, (b) restart with a drop ball or (c) caution the linesman?

3 A player collides heavily with a team-mate, but in retaliation he strikes an opponent by mistake. After sending him off do you restart with (a) a drop ball, (b) an indirect or (c) a direct free-kick?

4 You are cautioning a goalkeeper for time-wasting when he deliberately pushes an opponent with the ball. Do you (a) issue a second caution to the 'keeper, (b) order him off or (c) award a penalty instead of an indirect free-kick?

5

A: From the kick-off the ball is kicked directly into the opposing goal. You disallow the goal and award a goal-kick.

B: The goalkeeper quickly rolls the ball to a team-mate, who is outside the penalty-area, and collects it from the return pass.

C: Rolling the ball to the edge of the penalty-area, the 'keeper is about to kick it when he is charged fairly by an attacker. He does not release the ball when falling outside the area. You award a free-kick against the 'keeper.
(Where is the problem?)

ANSWERS

the correct manner. In A a goal-kick is the correct award because a goal cannot be scored direct from a place kick, i.e. the kick-off. In C the goalkeeper is penalised for handling the ball outside the area. He should have released it before falling outside the area.

1. The match must be abandoned (c) if the crossbar cannot be repaired or replaced with another (Law 1, decision 8). 2. Having (a) seen the incident you are not required to consider an alternative opinion of a neutral linesman. The penalty-kick must stand. 3. A direct free-kick (c) is the correct decision. 4. Any player (b) who is being cautioned then commits another cautionable offence must be sent off (Law 12, decision 2). 5. The problem is in B. The ball must be *kicked* from a goal-kick. It should be re-taken in

YOU ARE THE REF

compiled by STAN LOVER, Chairman of the London Referees' Society

1 An attacker is running in to take a penalty-kick when you see his team-mate being kicked by an opponent. The ball goes into the goal. After dismissing the offending player do you restart with (a) a kick-off (for the goal) or (b) have the penalty-kick retaken?

2 With five minutes to play fog descends. The score is 3-0. Do you (a) abandon the match, (b) wait in the hope that the match can continue or (c) award the match to the leading side?

3 A player complains that an opponent shouted without calling a name. Do you (a) caution the opponent, (b) take no action or (c) caution the player making the complaint?

4 You are cautioning a player who refuses to give his name. Do you (a) simply note his number, or (b) send him off?

5 A: From a corner-kick the kicker slices the ball directly out of play from the corner quadrant. You have the kick retaken.

B: When the ball is kicked it is headed back to the kicker, who is now in an offside position on the goal-line, by a defender. The ball touches the kicker and goes over the goal-line. You award a goal kick.

C: The goalkeeper places the ball only one yard from the goal-post, on the goal-line, to take the goal-kick. (Where is the problem?)

ANSWERS

1. The goal stands (a) because the offence occurred before the ball was in play and the reason for the penalty-kick is not affected. 2. Whenever possible a match should be played for the full period (b). If not it must be abandoned (a). 3. Take no action (b) if satisfied that the shout was not intended to distract an opponent. It is not necessary to call a name. 4. By refusing to give his name the player is committing further misconduct and must be dismissed (b). 5. The problem is in A. The correct decision is a goal-kick. In B the player who took the corner-kick cannot be offside because the ball was last played by a defender. In C there is no problem. The ball may be placed anywhere within the half of the six-yard goal-area nearest to where it crossed the goal-line.

24 AUGUST 1974

YOU ARE THE REF

compiled by STAN LOVER, Chairman of the London Referees' Society

1 A defender steps out of play over the goal-line (outside posts) to put an opponent offside. The ball is passed to the opponent who scores. Do you (a) award a free-kick for offside, (b) award a goal or (c) caution the defender and drop the ball?

2 After five minutes play you realise that one team has 12 players. Do you (a) abandon the match, (b) ask the captain to decide which player goes off or (c) abandon the match and start another?

3 When you are dropping the ball a player kicks wildly, misses the ball, but makes contact with an opponent. Do you (a) take no action, (b) award a free-kick or (c) re-drop the ball?

4 A goalkeeper catches the ball and then decides to sit on it. The ball immediately bursts. When you have obtained another ball do you (a) restart with a drop ball, (b) an indirect free-kick or (c) a direct free-kick?

5 When you inspect the pitch you find:

A: The length is 110 yards and the breadth is 70 yards.

B: Both the halfway flag posts are missing.

C: The goal-lines are not marked between the goal-posts.
(Where is the problem?).

ANSWERS

1. A goal should be awarded (b). The defender's action of leaving the pitch without permission must not be allowed to gain an advantage. 2. The match must be abandoned. It would be in order to start another match (c) with the correct number of players. The facts should be reported. 3. Award an indirect free-kick (b) for dangerous play. 4. Drop the ball (a). 5. The problem is in C.

The lines must be clearly marked between the posts and have the same width as the goalposts. In A the measurements are well within the limits, i.e. length 100-130 yards, breadth 50-100 yards. In B the halfway flagposts are optional equipment, but the corner posts are essential.

12 OCTOBER 1974

2 It's extra time as Hurst turns and lashes the ball which hits the underside of the bar, coming down and out again. The referee and linesmen confer. The outcome : a goal.

1 England, a goal down to West Germany, in the 1966 World Cup Final, are going forward yet again when Moore is brought down. The England captain takes the free-kick himself, lands it on the head of Geoff Hurst—and the scores are level.

BOBBY MOORE: Sir Alf Ramsey summed up Moore: "He's a great player and a great captain. One of the finest I've ever known. There is no one I would rather have in my side than Moore because I know he will always do a magnificent job for me."

GORDON BANKS: When England won 1966 World Cup, Banks was acclaimed as world's finest goalkeeper. Everything since has enhanced his claim to title.

JACK CHARLTON: At the final whistle in the 1966 Final, Big Jack fell to his knees, his face in his hands. He had given his all — and now he quietly shed tears of relief and pride : England were world champions.

MARTIN PETERS: Scored in both World Cup clashes with West Germany. Has occupied all 11 first team places, including emergency goalkeeper, in major football.

FAT ONES

Devised and drawn by Trevillion

3 In the dying seconds, Bobby Moore chests the ball down and lobs it through to Hurst, who races practically the length of the field before blasting the ball home—a hat-trick for Hurst and the World Cup for England.

ALAN BALL: England's outstanding player in 1966 World Cup Final. Automatic choice since. Perpetual-motion style has earned him admirers throughout the world.

1966 WORLD CUP FINAL

ENGLAND 4, WEST GERMANY 2.

Half-time: 1—1. 90-minute score: 2—2.

Scorers: England—Hurst (3), Peters. West Germany—Haller, Weber.

1 With only 20 minutes left of normal time in the 1970 World Cup quarter-final, England appear to be coasting through. Suddenly Beckenbauer's low 15-yard shot flies under Bonetti's body. It's 2—1 and Germany are back in the game.

...ght minutes are left as Seeler backheads the ball. ...floats over Bonetti and just under the bar for ...ctacular equaliser.

3 Extra time is a nightmare for England. After yet another defensive mix-up, Gerd Muller hammers the ball past Bonetti to shatter England's World Cup dream.

SEPP MAIER: Brave goalkeeping at Leon in 1970 helped West Germany gain revenge for defeat in 1966 World Cup Final.

1970 WORLD CUP QUARTER-FINAL

ENGLAND 2, WEST GERMANY 3.

Half-time: 1—0. 90-minute score: 2—2.

Scorers: England—Mullery, Peters.

West Germany—Beckenbauer, Seeler, Muller.

YOU ARE THE REF

● Compiled by STAN LOVER, Chairman of the London Referees' Society

1 You are given a match ball which (a) is 29 inches in circumference, (b) weighs 16 ozs. and (c) has a pressure of 15lb/sq. in. Which does not comply with the Law?

2 You have signalled a penalty-kick to be taken. The split-second before the ball is kicked you see an attacker hitting a defender. The ball finishes in the back of the net. The attacker is dismissed. Do you restart with (a) a free-kick, after disallowing the goal, (b) a retaken penalty or (c) kick-off for the goal?

3 When you restart play with a drop-ball a player plays the ball twice before another player touches it. Do you (a) re-drop the ball, (b) take no action, or (c) award a free-kick?

4 An attacker is in an offside position when he receives the ball direct from a throw-in. He is then tripped inside the penalty-area but manages to head the ball into the goal. Do you (a) award a goal, (b) a penalty-kick or (c) a free-kick for offside?

5

A: The ball is passed forward to an attacker in an offside position. Before you can stop the game the goalkeeper deflects the ball over the goal-line. You award a corner-kick.

B: From the corner the ball is caught by the goal keeper when he intentionally kicks out his leg dangerously close to an opponent's head. You award an indirect free-kick.

C: Although the ball is placed only six yards from goal you allow defenders to block the goal by standing on the line between the posts. (Where is the problem?)

ANSWERS

1. The ball is too large. It's circumference (a) must be between 27 and 28 inches. 2. Restart with a kick-off (c). The goal is awarded because the offence occurred before the ball was put into play from the penalty-kick. 3. Take no action (b). It is not an offence to play the ball twice when it is dropped to restart the game. 4. Award a goal (a). The attacker cannot be offside from a throw-in. Although tripped, normally a penalty-kick yards from the ball at a free-kick. is the only situation where defenders may stand less than ten kick the opponent was intentional. In A the attacker is not given offside because the ball is played by a defender. In C this ous play a penalty-kick should be awarded if the attempt to offence, you should allow the advantage in awarding the goal. 5. The problem is in B. Although the action could be danger-

30 NOVEMBER 1974

YOU ARE THE REF

compiled by STAN LOVER, Chairman of the London Referees' Society

1 A linesman signals a corner-kick but you decide a goal-kick is correct. He then throws down his flag in disgust. Do you (a) take no action, (b) change your decision or (c) change the linesman?

2 At a kick-off the ball hits your leg and returns to the kicker who passes it to a team-mate. Do you (a) retake the kick, (b) award a free-kick or (c) drop the ball?

3 Which is the correct size for a goal (a) 24ft x 8ft, (b) 28ft x 8ft or (c) 24ft x 8ft 6ins?

4 From a goal-kick the ball goes directly into the opposing half to an attacker standing in an offside position. He collects the ball and scores. Do you award (a) a goal, (b) a free-kick for offside or (c) retake the goal-kick?

5 A: Taking a throw-in a player loses his grip on the ball behind his head and it falls. You order him to retake the throw.

B: At the second attempt the thrower jumps with both feet off the ground just before releasing the ball. You again order the throw to be retaken.

C: From the third throw the ball is played back to the thrower by an attacking team-mate. The thrower is off the pitch but behind the opposing defenders. You stop play and award a free-kick for offside. (Where is the problem?)

ANSWERS

1. Linesmen must accept that the referee's decision is final. If not, an official committing an act of dissent should be replaced (c). 2. The kicker has played the ball twice and must be penalised by an indirect free-kick (b). 3. The correct size, measuring inside the posts, is 24ft x 8ft (a). 4. Award a goal (a) because a player cannot be offside from a goal-kick. 5. The problem is in B. The ball must be thrown with both feet on the ground. If not the throw is awarded to the opposing team. In A the decision to retake is correct because the ball was not thrown into play. In C the thrower is correctly given offside.

YOU ARE THE REF

1 From the kick-off the ball is kicked directly into the opponents' goal. Do you (a) award a goal, (b) have the kick retaken or (c) award a goal-kick?

● Compiled by STAN LOVER, Chairman of the London Referees' Society

2 Attempting to clear the ball a goalkeeper kicks it as an opponent challenges. The ball strikes the opponent's hand and is deflected to another attacker who scores. Do you (a) award a goal, (b) a goal-kick or (c) a free-kick for handling?

3 A substitute runs on to the pitch into his own team's penalty-area and kicks an opponent. You stop play and order him off. Do you then restart with (a) a drop ball, (b) an indirect free-kick or (c) a penalty?

4 Two players of the same team are arguing and pushing each other when standing inside their penalty-area. You stop the game to caution the players. Do you restart with (a) a penalty, (b) a drop ball or (c) an indirect free-kick?

5

A: A defender trips an opponent inside the penalty-area arc. You award a penalty-kick.

B: Time runs out just before the ball is placed for the penalty but you ignore this and allow the kick to be taken.

C: The ball is saved by the goalkeeper but rebounds to the penalty-taker who scores. You disallow the goal.
(Where is the problem?)

ANSWERS

1. Award a goal-kick (c). A goal cannot be scored direct from a kick-off. 2. Award a goal (a) because the ball was not intentionally handled by the attacker. 3. A penalty-kick (c). 4. Award an indirect free-kick (c) to the opponents for the defenders' ungentlemanly conduct. 5. The problem is in A. The arc is not part of the penalty-area. A direct free-kick should be awarded where the offence occurred. In B it is in order to extend time to allow a penalty-kick to be taken. In C the goal is not allowed because the match ends when the goalkeeper saves the ball.

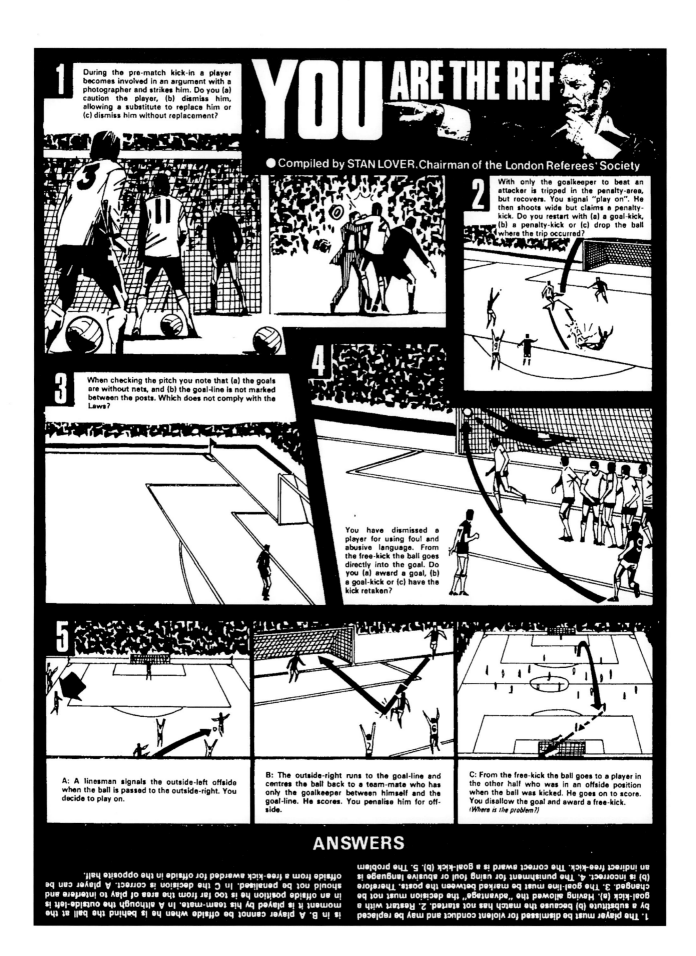

YOU ARE THE REF

1 During the pre-match kick-in a player becomes involved in an argument with a photographer and strikes him. Do you (a) caution the player, (b) dismiss him, allowing a substitute to replace him or (c) dismiss him without replacement?

● Compiled by STAN LOVER, Chairman of the London Referees' Society

2 With only the goalkeeper to beat an attacker is tripped in the penalty-area, but recovers. You signal "play on". He then shoots wide but claims a penalty-kick. Do you restart with (a) a goal-kick, (b) a penalty-kick or (c) drop the ball where the trip occurred?

3 When checking the pitch you note that (a) the goals are without nets, and (b) the goal-line is not marked between the posts. Which does not comply with the Laws?

4 You have dismissed a player for using foul and abusive language. From the free-kick the ball goes directly into the goal. Do you (a) award a goal, (b) a goal-kick or (c) have the kick retaken?

5

A: A linesman signals the outside-left offside when the ball is passed to the outside-right. You decide to play on.

B: The outside-right runs to the goal-line and centres the ball back to a team-mate who has only the goalkeeper between himself and the goal-line. He scores. You penalise him for offside.

C: From the free-kick the ball goes to a player in the other half who was in an offside position when the ball was kicked. He goes on to score. You disallow the goal and award a free-kick. *(Where is the problem?)*

ANSWERS

1. The player must be dismissed for violent conduct and may be replaced by a substitute (b) because the match has not started. 2. Restart with a goal-kick (a). Having allowed the "advantage" the decision must not be changed. 3. The goal-line must be marked between the posts. Therefore (b) is incorrect. 4. The punishment for using foul or abusive language is an indirect free-kick. The correct award is a goal-kick (b). 5. The problem is in B. A player cannot be offside when he is behind the ball at the moment it is played by his team-mate. In A although the outside-left is in an offside position he is too far from the area of play to interfere and should not be penalised. In C the decision is correct. A player can be offside from a free-kick awarded for offside in the opposite half.

31 MAY 1975

YOU ARE THE REF

● Compiled by STAN LOVER, Chairman of the London Referees' Society

1 From the kick-off the ball is passed, via three players, back to the goal-keeper. He misses the final pass and the ball goes into goal before an opponent has touched it. Do you (a) award a goal, (b) a corner-kick or (c) a goal-kick?

2 A trainer's bag, left on the pitch after treating a player, causes an opposing team's player to fall when in possession of the ball. Do you (a) take no action, (b) drop the ball or (c) award an indirect free-kick?

3 Tackling an opponent from behind a player attempts to play the ball but his boot makes contact with the opponent's leg. Do you (a) take no action, (b) award an indirect or (c) a direct free-kick?

4

A: From the kick-off the ball is played back directly to a defender. You stop play and award a free-kick.

B: Just before the free-kick is taken from the centre-spot an attacker runs ahead of the ball. You take no action.
(Where is the problem?)

ANSWERS

1. Award a goal (a). At least two players have touched the ball 2. Stop play, move the bag and restart with a drop ball (b). 3. Award an indirect free-kick (b). This action is considered to be dangerous play. 4. The problem is in A. The kick-off must be retaken and the ball kicked forward. In B there is no problem if a player is in front of the ball when the free-kick is awarded from the centre-spot.

SHOOT-IN AT STAN

Every week Stan Lover answers your letters on problems arising from the Laws of the Game.

BACK PASS?

Kevin Webb of Diss, Norfolk writes about an incident in a recent match. "I was about to take a throw-in when a team-mate suggested I should throw the ball at his back. This I did. The ball rebounded to me, I centred and a goal was scored. But, the referee disallowed the goal and gave a free-kick against me for ungentlemanly conduct.

"Why was this not treated in the same way as a pass from a team-mate?"

Kevin appreciates it would be wrong to throw the ball at an opponent, but does not see why he was penalised when a team-mate, who knew what was going on, was involved.

I can only assume the ref was not satisfied with the manner in which the ball was thrown at the team-mate. If it were thrown vigorously into the player's back the referee could have assumed there was some bad feeling between the two team-mates and, quite correctly, declared the action as "ungentlemanly conduct."

If it is made clear, to all, the tactic has been arranged and the second player simply turned his back to block the path of the ball, then there is no offence.

WHICH PENALTY-AREA?

An interesting question about penalty-kicks comes from M. Sheeran of Reigate, Surrey. "If an attacker kicks a defender in the opponent's penalty-area, when the ball is in play near the halfway line, should the ref award a free-kick where the offence took place or a penalty-kick against the attacker's side, i.e. at the other end?"

In putting this question M. Sheeran refers to the wording of Law 12 which says: "A penalty-kick can be awarded irrespective of the position of the ball, if in play, at the time an offence within the penalty-area is committed."

This could be misleading if it were not for the preceding paragraph, of this Law, which makes it clear a penalty-kick is only awarded if a direct free-kick offence is committed within the penalty-area by a player of the defending team.

In the above incident a direct free-kick should be awarded against the attacker and taken from inside the opponent's penalty-area, where the offence occurred.

HALF-TIME TEASER

"Can a team field eleven players without a goalkeeper?" was last week's teaser.

According to Law 3 (Number of players) the answer is NO! It specifies one of the players ". . . shall be the goalkeeper."

Can a competition rule that matches must be played for less than 90 minutes? Answer, next week.

YOU ARE THE REF

● Compiled by STAN LOVER, Chairman of the London Referees' Society

1 A goalkeeper is holding the ball near the edge of the penalty-area. An opponent charges him from behind and the 'keeper falls outside the area still clutching the ball. Do you (a) take no action, (b) award a free-kick against the 'keeper or (c) against the attacker?

2 You hear a linesman swearing at a player. Do you (a) take no action, (b) dismiss the linesman or (c) insist he apologises to the player?

3 The home team captain draws your attention to the stadium clock which indicates you have played 47 minutes in the first-half. Your watch records 44 minutes. Do you (a) stop play immediately or (b) play for one minute?

4

A: From a free-kick, outside the penalty-area, a defender passes the ball back to his goalkeeper. An opponent is more than ten yards away when the ball is kicked but has entered the penalty-area.

B: The goalkeeper attempts to throw the ball but it strikes the hand of the attacker and rebounds into the goal. You award a free-kick against the attacker. (Where is the problem?)

ANSWERS

1. Award a direct free-kick against the attacker (c) for the offence of charging from behind. 2. Dismiss the linesman (b). 3. Provided your watch has not stopped play should continue for one minute (b). After all, the stadium clock could be wrong or you could have allowed time for injuries etc. 4. The problem is in B. A goal should be allowed because the attacker did not intentionally handle the ball. In A there is no problem because the free-kick is outside the penalty-area and the attacker was at least ten yards from the ball.

13 DECEMBER 1975

YOU ARE THE REF

● Compiled by STAN LOVER, Chairman of the London Referees' Society

1 From a throw-in the ball bounces outside the touchline and then into play. Do you (a) take no action, (b) have the throw-in retaken or (c) award a throw-in to the opposing team?

2 Before a match you see a player inserting contact lenses into his eyes. Do you (a) take no action or (b) refuse to allow him to play?

3 From a goal-kick the ball is passed towards a defender but it is intercepted by an attacker who is outside the penalty-area. He has only the goalkeeper between himself and the goal-line. He scores. Do you (a) allow the goal or (b) award a free-kick for offside?

4 A: Time is extended for a penalty-kick. The defending team's captain wants to change his goalkeeper to face the kick but, as this would cause delay, you refuse permission.

B: The goalkeeper then strikes an opponent and is sent-off. You allow another player to take his place for the penalty-kick.

(Where is the problem?)

ANSWERS

1. Have the throw-in retaken (b) because the ball did not enter the field at the place where it went out of play. 2. Take no action (a). Contact lenses are not considered to be dangerous to the wearer or to opponents. 3. Allow the goal (a) because the attacker was behind the ball from the goal-kick. 4. The problem is in A. It is in order for the goalkeeper to be changed at any time, after notifying the referee. In B the goalkeeper is correctly dismissed and time is allowed for another player to go into goal.

SHOOT-IN AT STAN

Every week Stan Lover answers your letters on problems arising from all aspects of the Laws of the game.

Several readers have enquired about various aspects of football and refereeing which involve administration. Typical of these letters is that from Malcolm Snow of Warley, West Midlands.

"Please advise the address of the Football Association. I would like to ask a few questions and obtain a copy of their rules and Laws."

Two addresses which may be helpful to readers are:—

(a) THE FOOTBALL ASSOCIATION,
(The Secretary)
16 LANCASTER GATE,
LONDON W2 3LW.

(b) THE REFEREES' ASSOCIATION,
(Hon. General Secretary)
135 BARROWS LANE,
BIRMINGHAM B26 1SE.

Malcolm asks a specific question, "How are referees selected for the World Cup and are all travelling expenses paid?"

World Cup officials are selected by the Referees' Committee of F.I.F.A. For the 1974 Final tournament in West Germany F.I.F.A. chose 30 referees. Eleven were from the Finalist countries, 19 from the rest of the World. Every member country of F.I.F.A. (there are 142 national associations) may nominate seven officials for the F.I.F.A. Referees' List for international, Olympic, and World Cup matches.

All travel and accommodation expenses are paid either by F.I.F.A. or by the home national association, depending on the type of match.

CHECK LIST

For a school project Simon Hill of Hemel Hempstead, Herts, asks for a list of the items a referee must have for each game.

The essentials are:—watch, whistle, book, pencil, and a coin. What is missing? Surprisingly, many trainee referees forget to add a ball!

HALF-TIME TEASER

"Should a referee take any action if he sees a goalkeeper sitting on the crossbar?" was last week's teaser.
ANSWER: Yes. This is considered to be an act of ungentlemanly conduct for which the offender can expect to be cautioned.

Many readers may recall the case of the Irish goalkeeper who was sent off for repeating this offence. The culprit found out the hard way that sitting on the crossbar is no joke — Irish or otherwise!

This week, a question which is not as difficult as it may seem.

When must a goalkeeper be penalised for handling the ball in a penalty-area?

24 APRIL 1976

YOU ARE THE REF

● Compiled by STAN LOVER, Chairman of the London Referees' Society

1 A goalkeeper throws the ball over an opponent's head, takes six steps to run past him to catch the ball before releasing it after a further three steps. Do you (a) take no action, (b) award an indirect, or (c) a direct free-kick?

2 A player wearing a turban manages to trap the ball in it. He then runs 20 yards with the ball into the goal. Do you (a) award a goal, (b) an indirect free-kick or (c) drop the ball? (This incident actually happened in a junior match in England!)

3 From a goal-kick the ball is stopped on the penalty-area boundary-line by an attacker. He scores. Do you (a) award a goal, (b) have the goal-kick retaken or (c) a free-kick against the attacker?

4 LEAVE IT!

A: From a shot at goal the ball hits the crossbar and rebounds towards two attackers who have no defenders nearby. One attacker shouts, "Leave it!" to the other and kicks the ball into goal. You disallow the goal, caution the scorer and award an indirect free-kick.

B: Before the free-kick is taken you recognise the scorer as a player whom you sent-off in a match the previous week. However, you decide to take no action.

(Where is the problem?)

ANSWERS

1. Award an indirect free-kick (b). 2. Award an indirect free-kick (b) for an act of ungentlemanly conduct. 3. Have the goal-kick retaken (b) because the ball did not completely cross the boundary-line and was not in play when stopped by the attacker. 4. The problem is in A. It is not an offence to shout, "Leave it!" unless the shout is intended to distract an opponent. In this case no opposing player was involved. The goal should stand. In B it is correct to take no action. Your report submitted on the previous incident will be actioned by the appropriate authority.

SHOOT-IN AT STAN

The application of ADVANTAGE in soccer still causes some confusion. Alan Owen writes from Port Talbot, W. Glamorgan.

"When I was running, with the ball, along the touch-line, a defender brought me down with a rugby-type tackle. I managed to continue and took the ball around the goalkeeper. I chipped the ball over the head of a defender, on the goal-line. He handled it trying to prevent a goal but it went into the net.

"The referee called play back to the point where I was brought down and awarded a free-kick.

"My point is, if the referee had played the advantage he should have awarded a penalty-kick or, by playing advantage twice, a goal. Can this be done?"

I last commented, on the ADVANTAGE LAW, in my SHOOT-IN column of 25th October, 1975. As a reminder I quote from Law 5(b). It says the referee shall, "refrain from penalising in cases where he is satisfied that, by doing so, he would be giving an advantage to the offending team."

There is no restriction to the number of times advantage may be applied i.e. as in the case quoted by Alan Owen, two, three or more incidents can occur, consecutively, which, if penalised immediately would give an advantage to the offending team. Play should be allowed to continue, the referee has power to deal with offending players (by caution or dismissal) after the particular phase of play has been completed. In the above example a goal could have been awarded.

The only explanation for the referee's action which occurs to me is the referee signalled the free-kick for the first offence before realising 'advantage was on' and the signal was not heard by Alan.

It does happen, from time to time, that referees signal too quickly before assessing advantage situations.

It also happens that an apparent advantage arises because defenders have heard the signal, ease off opponents or handle the ball for the free-kick.

Two points should be stressed. First, if the referee has stopped play he has no power to change that decision.

Secondly, the referee is not permitted to change his mind if he allows play to continue and the team offended against does not benefit.

HALF-TIME TEASER

Animal lovers, and probably the R.S.P.C.A., may be anxious to learn the answer to last week's teaser about the player who kicks a dog which has entered the field of play.

It all depends on the circumstances. Action could be taken against a player for assault on an innocent intruder but not for an act of self-defence.

This week's problem is — can a substitute play in a number 13 shirt?

15 MAY 1976

YOU ARE THE REF

● Compiled by STAN LOVER, Chairman of the London Referees' Society

1 At a penalty-kick the kicker runs to the ball but instead of kicking it he passes his foot over the top. The goalkeeper is deceived into moving from his line. When the ball is kicked he stops it two yards out of the goal. Do you (a) take no action, (b) award a free-kick to the defending team or (c) have the penalty-kick retaken?

2 An attacker has a clear run to goal. The goalkeeper runs out of the penalty-area and brings down the attacker with a rugby-style tackle. Do you (a) caution the 'keeper and restart with a direct free-kick, (b) caution and award a penalty-kick or (c) dismiss the 'keeper and award a direct free-kick?

3 A player plays the ball twice after it is dropped. Do you (a) take no action, (b) re-drop the ball or (c) award an indirect free-kick?

4

A: A substitute runs onto the field and pushes an opponent. You stop play, caution the sub and award an indirect free-kick.

B: The play is stopped for one minute while dealing with the incident. Although no player has been injured you allow one minute at the end of the half.

(Where is the problem?)

ANSWERS

1. Order the penalty-kick to be retaken (c) after cautioning the kicker for ungentlemanly conduct. 2. Dismiss the goalkeeper (c) for serious foul-play and restart with a direct free-kick. 3. Take no action (a). There is no offence in playing the ball twice when it is dropped by the referee. 4. The problem is in A. The correct method of restarting play, after cautioning the sub, is with a direct free-kick for the pushing offence. In B it is correct to allow time lost for any cause at the discretion of the referee.

3 JULY 1976

YOU ARE THE REF

● Compiled by STAN LOVER, Chairman of the London Referees' Society

1 A player with an injured arm throws the ball in with his good arm from behind and over his head. Do you (a) take no action, (b) have the throw retaken or (c) award a throw-in to the opposing team?

2 Just after the kick-off players from both teams complain that the ball is out of shape. During a stoppage, you examine the ball. It is out of shape but you are satisfied that the size and pressure are correct. Should you (a) continue, (b) change the ball at half-time or (c) immediately?

3 From a corner-kick the ball is kicked along the goal-line. A spectator moves onto the field and deflects the ball to an attacker who scores. Should you (a) award a goal, (b) drop the ball where the spectator touched it or (c) have the corner-kick retaken?

4
A: You have just blown your whistle to end the first-half when a defender, in his own penalty-area, strikes an opponent. You dismiss the defender and extend time for the penalty-kick.

B: You then find that the penalty-spot has not been marked. You decide to pace 12 yards from the centre of the goal and have the kick taken without an official marking.

(Where is the problem?)

ANSWERS . . .

1. **Law 15 — Throw-in** — states that the ball must be thrown-in with both hands. If not a throw-in is awarded to the opposing team. 2. Change the ball immediately (c). Although weight and pressure are in order the ball must be spherical. 3. The ball must be dropped (b) at the place where the spectator touched it. 4. The problem is in A.

Having blown your whistle it is incorrect to then extend play for a penalty-kick to be taken. In B there is no problem. Your estimate of the penalty-spot position would be acceptable. But, the moral is — check field markings before starting every match.

SHOOT-IN AT STAN

"I'm fed up!" writes Tony Brent of Richmond, Surrey. "I am a Queens Park Rangers supporter and am fed up with the postponements of important matches at Loftus Road due to bad weather. I look forward all week to my Saturday match. The weekend is not the same if my game is off. Also I can't always get to the match at a later date because it is usually an evening kick-off.

"I expect fans of other teams feel as I do when their games are postponed. When can we expect guaranteed football on artificial turf?"

The simple answer, Tony, is because of lack of money. The cost of a full-size soccer pitch would be over £¼ million. Only a handful of clubs could find this kind of finance. Until all clubs, in the Football League, could afford artificial pitches, it is unlikely that the League would allow their matches to be played on this type of surface.

One argument is that teams playing on their own artificial pitches, would have an advantage over visiting clubs who play on the traditional grass/mud surfaces. A counter to this is that the "artificial" teams would be at a disadvantage when playing away!

There is no problem with the Laws of the game because Law 1 — THE FIELD OF PLAY, does not specify the type of surface on which the game must be played.

This point is confirmed by the fact that World Cup matches have been played on artificial turf. F.I.F.A. News reports that the first such match was played, on 24th September, 1976, between Canada and the U.S.A. at the Empire Stadium, Vancouver. Result was 1-1.

These events mark an historic beginning to a new trend for football throughout the world. Of course, we will lose some of the excitement of the traditional British winter type game, but, having seen matches played on artificial surfaces, I think we will see new skills and techniques developing which will be just as exciting to watch.

Pitches which can be used 24 hours a day, seven days a week, will provide vast opportunities for young players to develop these new skills and techniques.

Like Tony Brent, I too am fed up when I have to call off a game due to weather problems.

HALF-TIME TEASER

"Do linesmen check players' boots after the half-time interval?" was last week's teaser.

Answer: No. Law 4, Decision No. 8, instructs referees to inspect players' footwear ... "prior to the start of the game." However, referees have the power to inspect at any time if necessary.

This week a simple question on offside.

A player is in an offside position when the ball is passed towards him by a team-mate. What can he do to put himself onside?

2 APRIL 1977

YOU ARE THE REF

● Compiled by STAN LOVER, Chairman of the London Referees' Society

1 When the ball is in play a player asks for permission to leave the field. You agree. Before he reaches the touchline he intercepts the ball and scores. Do you (a) allow the goal, (b) drop the ball or (c) award a free-kick to the opposing team?

2 A player is about to take a throw-in when he is kicked, standing outside the touch-line, by an opponent. After dismissing the offender do you restart with (a) a throw-in, (b) a drop ball or (c) a direct free-kick?

3 A player commits two direct free-kick offences at the same time by handling the ball and tripping an opponent. Do you (a) simply award a direct free-kick, (b) caution the player for ungentlemanly conduct and award an indirect free-kick or (c) caution and award a direct free-kick?

4

A: A goalkeeper catches the ball and then rolls it towards the edge of the penalty-area. He follows it taking eight steps before he picks up the ball.

B: He then throws it, and, with the aid of a strong wind, the ball goes to the other end, into the goal, without touching another player. You award a goal-kick. (Where is the problem?)

ANSWERS

1. The player should be cautioned and an indirect free-kick awarded (c). (International Board answer). 2. The game must be restarted with a throw-in (a) because the offence occurred when the ball was not in play. 3. The offender should be cautioned for ungentlemanly conduct and a direct free-kick awarded (c). 4. The problem is in B. The correct award is a goal (Law 10). In A there is no problem because the goalkeeper has released the ball while taking eight steps.

SHOOT-IN AT STAN

Every week Stan Lover answers your letters on problems arising from all aspects of the Laws of the Game.

PLAYING FOR ENGLAND

"Do you agree," writes Ted Drennan of Stourbridge, Worcester, "that any player who has been sent-off should not be allowed to play for England?" Ted provides names of players whose record of misconduct, in the Football League and at international level, leaves a lot to be desired.

Ted ends his letter by making the point: "This policy could have an enormous influence on the way football is played, by encouraging sporting behaviour. Perhaps we could then look to our national team with more pride."

I am sure that the misconduct records of potential international players are studied before names are listed for selection. No player is likely to be considered seriously if his record suggests that he could be sent-off in the opening minutes of a vital match.

Other players, with less serious misconduct records, but with outstanding skill, may be listed with the knowledge of the risks involved in having such players in the side.

Ideally, the international squad should be chosen from players with outstanding skill and unblemished conduct. There was a day when the Football Association confirmed this policy by issuing the following notice to all senior amateur clubs:

"The Football Association Amateur Selection Committee is gravely concerned about the increasing amount of unfair play and misconduct in amateur football. It has therefore been decided that no player will be considered for selection in any F.A. Representative XI or International team who has herein after been found guilty of misconduct.

"The committee will review each case from time to time and will note whether subsequent conduct has justified reconsideration."

The above notice was issued in 1968. Alas, the England Amateur team no longer exists, but I am sure that those who formulated the policy have tried to maintain a balance between their ideals and the harsh facts of modern competitive play. Obviously though, not to the satisfaction of Ted Drennan, his views can serve to remind us all that football is a sport intended to be played by and for sportsmen.

HALF-TIME TEASER

How long should the referee suspend play before abandoning a match? The answer to last week's teaser cannot be quantified in minutes. It is left to the referee's discretion.

This week Mark Hoggard of Huggate, York, asks: "Have the linesmen the power to dismiss a referee who, in their judgment, is biased towards one of the teams?"

Answer in June 4th issue.

Write to Stan Lover: SHOOT!, IPC Magazines Ltd., King's Reach Tower, Stamford Street, London SE1 9LS.

21 MAY 1977

YOU ARE THE REF

● Compiled by STAN LOVER, Chairman of the London Referees' Society

1 As a player is about to take a penalty-kick a defender shouts "miss it". The ball is kicked but misses the goal. After you have cautioned the defender do you restart with (a) another penalty-kick, (b) a goal-kick or (c) a free-kick to the attacking side?

MISS IT!

2 At a corner-kick, (a) two attackers stand within ten yards of the ball, (b) the ball is placed on the corner quadrant line and (c) you refuse to allow the kicker to remove a corner-post. Which is incorrect?

3 A defender, in his own penalty-area, objects strongly to a decision. You stop play to caution him for showing dissent. Do you restart with (a) a penalty-kick, (b) an indirect free-kick or (c) a drop ball?

4

A: You send-off a player during the first-half because of dangerous studs. The player's captain wants to introduce a substitute but you refuse because the first player has been sent-off.

B: At the start of the second-half you notice that the first player has returned to his team. When the ball is out of play you caution him but allow him to continue in the match.

(Where is the problem?)

ANSWERS

1. Restart by having the penalty-kick retaken (a). 2. The incorrect action is (b). The ball must be placed within the quadrant. 3. Restart play with an indirect free-kick (b). 4. The problem is in A. The first player may be substituted if required. In B the player may continue in the match but should be cautioned for returning to play before checking with you that his equipment has been corrected.

Every week Stan Lover answers your letters on problems arising from all aspects of the Laws of the Game.

ANOTHER UNFAIR KICK

A few weeks ago I commented on the Donkey Kick. Steve Henshaw of Wolverhampton writes: "I saw George Best and Rodney Marsh try a similar type of kick when Fulham played Hereford last September.

"Best put one foot under the ball and placed a hand on the top of it, in effect, pressing it to his foot. He then lifted the ball and removed his hand when it reached about knee-height. Rodney Marsh then volleyed the ball towards goal.

"In this case, the referee awarded a free-kick against Best. Was this the correct decision?"

Bearing in mind the decision of the International F.A. Board that, in the case of a Donkey Kick, ". . . the ball was not kicked in the accepted sense of the word," and the definition of a kick being: ". . . a blow with the foot," the George Best method could not be interpreted as a fair kick at the ball.

The free-kick should have been retaken. It is possible the referee concerned considered Best had handled the ball. However, I could not support this interpretation because the ball was not in play.

Whatever the reasoning the moral of the various incidents discussed is that unorthodox methods of putting the ball into play are likely to come unstuck and result, as in the case of George Best, in the referee deciding to penalise such methods.

I read somewhere a kick could be described mathematically as: ". . . an impulse which is Force f multiplied by Delta t (an immeasurable length of time). If the ball is lifted the foot is in contact for a measurable length of time. It is not an impulse and is therefore not a kick."

My impulse, on reading this technical definition, is to say to all players who are delegated to take free-kicks: "Don't try to be too clever, keep it simple. Kick the ball into play."

HALF-TIME TEASER

Last week I asked what the referee's decision would be if both teams wanted to change ends at half-time without an interval.

ANSWER: The referee has to agree. While players have the right to an interval it is not compulsory. All players must agree to forego the interval.

The poor ref has no option, even if he feels HE needs an interval!

This week Tom Drennan of Belfast, poses the teaser: "Is a trainer allowed to leave a wet sponge with a player who has been treated for injury?"

Write to Stan Lover: SHOOT, IPC Magazines Ltd., King's Reach Tower, Stamford Street, London SE1 9LS.

25 JUNE 1977

YOU ARE THE REF

Compiled by CLIVE THOMAS

1 If a ground is covered with snow, but the lines are cleared by the groundsmen, should you play the match?

2 You award a free-kick and decide to warn the offender. You walk to him but the player refuses and walks away. What should you do ... (a) nothing and get on with play, (b) run after the player and then warn him or (c) ensure the player comes to you?

3 A goalkeeper in his own goal-area, obstructs an opponent to prevent him reaching the ball. The opponent charges the 'keeper fairly. Should you award ...(a) a free-kick against the attacker or (b) play on?

4 From a kick-off the centre-forward kicks the ball directly into the opposing goal, should you award ... (a) a goal or (b) goal-kick?

5 A player taking a throw-in, throws the ball correctly but with both feet off the ground. The ball goes straight into his opponents' goal, should you award...(a) a goal or (b) throw to opponents?

ANSWERS

1. No. These last few weeks, referee's decisions on inspection of grounds have been so important and there is a lot of pressure put on referees with the TV media and supporters. The referee's first job is to ensure the ground is safe to the players; I suggest he runs about with a football and the apprentices from the local club, after that the referee can say if it is not dangerous or too bad to play on. 2. Ensure the player comes to you (c). Referees run after players too often. To me it shows complete disrespect for authority. I remember refereeing Holland and Czechoslovakia in the European Championship finals in Yugoslavia and one of the players from Holland, after being cautioned, walked away from me in the centre of the field and refused to accept I had given him the yellow card. I asked him twice to come to me, he refused, I then showed him the red card 3. Play on (b). 4. Goal-kick (b) 5. Throw to opponents (b).

The real culprit does not always go down in the referee's book. Artist PAUL TREVILLION explains why.

A. FAKING A BUTT. As the forward takes the ball past the defender, his shirt is grabbed. As he shakes himself free the defender falls to the ground complaining he has been butted.

B. FALSIFYING A CHARGE. Here the forward shifts his weight to his outside foot, so unbracing himself before more bodily contact occurs. The defender's moment of challenge is the forward's cue to hurl himself to the ground. A convincing act gives the defender a booking.

C. PROVOCATIVE PAT. After taking the legs from under a player, the offender moves in to offer an apparently apologetic pat on the cheek. It looks friendly but it can be a blatant provocation when the hand is held rigid, giving a jarring rap, sufficient to evoke retaliation.

D. THE KIDNEY JAB. A player helped to his feet after a fall is open to this. Again it looks friendly, but the thumbs are buried in the kidneys. Retaliation always follows.

YOU ARE THE REF

Compiled by CLIVE THOMAS

1. A player uses foul and abusive language to the referee who promptly sends him off the field. From the free-kick the ball goes directly into the goal, should you award (a) a goal or (b) a goal-kick?

2. The pitch markings are not clear when both teams go off at half-time. Have you the power to ask the groundsman to remark the field?

3. A player went off the field with the referee's permission through injury, but returns without a signal and goes on to score. Should you (a) award a goal, (b) a caution and a goal-kick or (c) a caution and an indirect free-kick?

4. Taking a goal-kick, a 'keeper follows the ball outside the area, taps it back, and then clears. Should you award an indirect free-kick?

5. An attacker gives a through pass for his colleague, who is just outside the penalty-area, when a defender deliberately catches the ball. Should you caution the player and award a direct free-kick?

ANSWERS

1. A goal-kick (b). 2. Yes. You will usually find at most Football League grounds the groundsman is awaiting the referee at the end of the tunnel. In a recent match between Millwall and Luton at The Den, the touch-lines could not be seen through mud. Immediately the groundsmen cleared them during the interval. Not many appreciate the invaluable work these people do to ensure the match is played. 3. A caution and a goal-kick (b). 4. Yes. 5. Yes. In my Millwall and Luton match, a similar thing happened with a Millwall attack. It gave me no option but to caution Donaghy, of Luton, who accepted the decision with no question.

Missed penalties

What is the greatest number of penalties missed by one side in a single game?

ANDY MIDGLEY, PETERBOROUGH

● As far as the Football League is concerned, Andy, it's three.
Manchester City missed all three awarded to them in a First Division game against Newcastle on 27th January, 1912.
Earlier, on 13th February, 1909, Burnley missed three out of four in a Second Division game against Grimsby.

Charlton v. Villa

I have a very old programme for a Fifth Round F.A. Cup-tie between Charlton and Aston Villa on 12th February, 1938, and would like to know what happened?

STEVE ELLIOTT, BROADSTAIRS

● For a start, Steve, a club-record attendance of 75,031 packed The Valley that pre-War afternoon. But there was no immediate decisive result. That game ended 1-1, the replay at Villa Park 2-2 — and it took a third meeting at neutral Highbury to sort it out 4-1 in Villa's favour.

Fastest hat-trick

Who's scored the fastest hat-trick in the Football or Scottish League?

KEVIN CAMERON, ROSS-SHIRE

● Almost a dozen have had their three goals in three-minutes-flat, Kevin — but the fastest I can find is the two-and-a-half-minute threesome by Jimmy Scarth for Gillingham v. Orient in a Division Three (South) game on 1st November, 1952.
And, in full international football, it will be pretty good going if anyone ever beats the three-and-a-half-minute hat-trick by Tottenham's Willie Hall for England v. Ireland at Old Trafford on 16th November, 1938.
What's more, Hall went on to get five in England's 7-0 win.

Youngest

Who's the youngest player to score in a Football League game?

ROBERT LEACH, AUSTRALIA

● Ronnie Dix holds that record, Robert.
He was 15 years and 180 days old when he scored for Bristol Rovers v. Norwich in a Third Division (South) match on 3rd March, 1928.
Dix later played for Blackburn, Villa, and Derby in the First Division — and made his full England debut just before World War Two broke out.

Five in debut

Which player has scored the most goals on his Football League debut?

ANDREW LEOPOLD, LEATHERHEAD

● Chelsea's George Hilsdon — who later gained eight England caps — takes that one, Andrew.
He scored five for the club against Glossop, in Division Two, on 1st September, 1906.
In Scotland, the record for a League debutant is three better at eight — by John Dyet, for King's Park v. Forfar, in a Division Two game on 2nd January, 1930.

Final hat-trick

Has anyone ever scored a hat-trick in a an F.A. Cup Final?

JOHN CAWLEY, Co. TYRONE

● Yes, John, three Final strikers have struck that hard.
The last was Stan Mortensen in Blackpool's dramatic 4-3 "injury-time" victory over Bolton in 1953 — the match in which Matthews got his Cup-winners' medal at last.
Some records credit one of the three as an own-goal to Hassall — but the deflection was really limited enough not to deprive "Morty" of his glory.
The other two three-goal men were long before — Townley in Blackburn's 6-1 defeat of Sheffield Wednesday in 1890; and Logan in Notts County's 4-1 victory over Bolton in 1894.

17 MARCH 1979

THE UPS AND DOWNS OF

MARK McGHEE

THE soccer career of Aberdeen's recent £65,000 signing from Newcastle, has had more ups and downs than an overworked elevator.

McGhee, only 24, must feel like a champion surfer who can do no wrong one day and little right the next.

"I wanted to be a success with Newcastle," says McGhee, "but I don't think I really got the opportunity to show my best form at St. James' Park.

"For a start I was played out of position and that didn't help my game. With Morton I was allowed to drift around the wings and I scored a lot of my goals from this position, cutting in from the touch-line and having a go.

"Newcastle must have been impressed because they paid out £150,000 for me . . . and then changed my game!

"They wanted me to play as a sort of target man and that role really doesn't suit me."

The talented McGhee must have been feeling low because this was his second attempt to parade his skills in front of English audiences.

Declined

The player was a brilliant prospect as a schoolboy and several Scottish clubs wanted him to sign, but he declined their offers and headed for Ashton Gate, home of Bristol City.

Things, however, didn't work out. He says: "Quite simply, I got homesick. Oh, I know I was hardly a million miles away, but still I wanted to get home.

"Bristol City, thankfully, understood the situation and gave me a free transfer and I was back in Scotland as swiftly as I could make it."

McGhee might have been a bit disappointed at failing to make it big with Bristol City, but that dejection changed to delight with the news that Celtic were taking an interest.

He played several trials for the club and the then manager Jock Stein is reported to have been impressed. Then things went wrong again for McGhee.

Scotland supremo Stein was involved in his unfortunate car accident four years ago and it took him a season to recover. With Stein out of action McGhee's name slipped out of Celtic's attention.

The call-up to Parkhead never arrived and McGhee drifted into junior football. Morton, though, were quick to spot his immense potential and manager Benny Rooney, never afraid to give youth its chance, brought McGhee into his first team.

He formed a devastating partnership with Andy Ritchie as Morton demoralised oppositions with montonous regularity on their way to the First Division title.

McGhee didn't finish the season with a title-winning team . . . he ended up with a side being relegated.

Newcastle, hurtling at a phenomenal pace into the Second Division, tried to halt the nose dive by spending £150,000 on McGhee and £100,000 on Clydebank striker Mike Larnach. The gamble didn't pay off and, ironically, Larnach is also back in Scotland after joining Motherwell earlier in the season for £60,000.

So, McGhee was down again. Fortunately, it seems, not for long. He signed for Aberdeen just before the League Cup Final and would have certainly made history if he had been given a substitute's role and The Dons had won the trophy. He would have been the only player in the game to have picked up a winner's medal without even playing one minute's football in the tournament.

As it turns out, McGhee wasn't risked and Rangers went out to win the Cup with a last-minute goal from Colin Jackson. "It was so close that day," says McGhee. "I felt the disappointment just like every other Aberdeen player. They fought so hard they really deserved something better at the end of the day.

"Anyway, I'm delighted to be at Pittodrie. My former boss at Morton, Benny Rooney, thinks a lot of Dons manager Alex Ferguson and after only a couple of weeks in his company I can understand why.

"Aberdeen are going places and I don't want anything to interrupt my progress this time . . ."

YOU ARE THE REF
Compiled by CLIVE THOMAS

1 A white line has been added to the goal-line to mark the centre of the goal. Is this allowed?

2 A player runs over the goal-line and crashes into the wall that surrounds the pitch. Should you stop play whilst he receives treatment?

3 Should you allow the captain who wins the toss to choose to kick-off instead of selecting a half to defend (a) yes or (b) no?

4 From a corner-kick the ball strikes you and is deflected over the goal-line, should you award (a) another corner, (b) have the kick retaken, (c) a goal-kick or (d) a drop-ball at the place where it struck you?

5 A defender trips an opponent inside the penalty arc. Should you award (a) a penalty or (b) a direct free-kick?

ANSWERS

1. No. I have found in some matches abroad that this line is put in by groundsmen. Luckily I have seen this when inspecting the ground on the morning of the match and immediately told the groundsmen to remove it. 2. No, although I believe the referee should at least call the trainer to the injured player. 3. Yes (a). 4. A goal-kick (c). 5. A direct free-kick (b).

12 MAY 1979

Gates UP in lower Divisions

HAVE you been taking a check on the gates lately? No — well you should because it appears that a very interesting trend is emerging.

For some strange, ambiguous reason the big guns of the First Division are losing customers, and their hitherto poor little brothers down in the lower reaches are gaining them.

Study the evidence. Over the first five-match period of the season First Division crowds slumped by a total of 181,931, Second Division gates were down by the comparatively meaningless figure of 17,741, yet Third Division attendances were up by 41,242 and Fourth Division crowds by 14,678.

Crowded

Those figures are quite significant and prompt the suggestion that folk have got a little fed up of risking life and limb on the crowded terraces of the bigger club and are turning back for their Saturday afternoon entertainment to the local team — perhaps the one they sacrificed years ago when travelling became so much easier.

Only four First Division clubs recorded improved gates over the period in question. Arsenal (whose visitors were Ipswich and Manchester United), Middlesbrough (who went to the top of the League briefly after beating Manchester City), West Bromwich Albion (despite a wretched start) and Wolves.

On the other hand Tottenham, who like Albion bit the dust with a vengeance, suffered a fall in their average gate of around 18,000 . . . the actual figures 40,853 to 22,872.

As an illustration of what was going on a couple of Divisions beneath them, just look at Barnsley. Despite a hesitant start to their new Third Division status the Oakwell side pulled in 43,399 people for three home games, an average of nearly 15,000.

Both Sheffield clubs, operating together in the Third Division for the first time ever, have been consistently getting five-figure gates.

Good for the little 'uns. Perhaps the ace up their sleeve is the admission fee.

You can still have a Saturday afternoon match for the modest sum of £1.50 if you're willing to restrict yourself to the lower Divisions, but it can cost you a pretty packet if you insist on watching the best. And with top clubs playing three matches a week at the moment that is very restrictive to the average family man.

Hence maybe Liverpool getting only 35,000 for their very attractive European Cup-tie against Dinamo Tbilisi, and traditionally well supported clubs like Everton and Manchester City struggling to top the 30,000 mark.

Maybe the fact that there has been no televised soccer on a Sunday, thus the loss of opportunity for fans to at least see one of their local clubs on the box, has attributed too to the effect on gates in the regions, but whatever the reason it is a trend that will be watched with interest by boards of directors all over the country.

NICK STEPHENS

Fans packed the terraces for Barnsley's Third Division game with Sheffield Wednesday in August.

YOU ARE THE REF

Compiled by CLIVE THOMAS

1 A groundsman asks the referee if he may mark lines on the pitch with creosote. Are you right to agree?

2 When taking a throw-in a player lifts one foot off the ground. Should you (a) take no action, (b) award a throw-in to the opposite side or (c) allow the throw-in to be taken again?

3 A player's boot flies off when he is about to kick the ball. Should you (a) order him off to replace it, (b) stop play or (c) allow him to replace it while play proceeds?

4 A player with the ball deliberately turns his back on an opponent when he is about to be tackled, and the opponent charges him fairly from behind. Should you award (a) a direct free-kick against the opponent, or (b) take no action?

5 A defender in his own penalty-area attempts to kick an opponent but does not make contact. Should you (a) award an indirect free-kick, (b) take no action or (c) award a penalty-kick?

ANSWERS

1. No. We have just had the case of a Welsh rugby star playing in a match where some burning substance was used to mark the field. Unfortunately it went on to the player's body and the player had to be treated for burns. 2. Award a throw-in to the opposing side (b). 3. allow him to replace it while play proceeds (c). 4. Take no action (b). 5. Award a penalty-kick (c).

19 MAY 1979

YOU ARE THE REF

Compiled by CLIVE THOMAS

1 Is it compulsory to have halfway line flags?

2 When are trainers allowed to come on to the pitch? (a) When a player is injured or (b) only when the referee signals?

3

4 From a goal-kick, the ball strikes you before it leaves the penalty-area, and an attacker runs in and kicks the ball into the goal. Should you (a) award a goal or (b) have the goal-kick retaken?

5 The ball slips from the hands of a player who is taking a throw-in. Should you (a) allow him to take it again or (b) award the throw-in to the opponents?

During a match a player is showing by the disgruntled expression on his face, he disagrees with you. Should you (a) take no action or (b) caution the player?

ANSWERS

1. No. In some televised matches, producers sometimes ask me if I would not mind the flags removed as they are in front of cameras. I have always co-operated in this matter. 2. Only when the referee signals (b). Unfortunately a few trainers called on to the field to treat an injured player, start haranguing the opposition before attending to the injured player. This type of trainer needs to be warned in no uncertain manner. 3. Caution the captain said nothing against my decisions, 'but it looks could kill'. I warned him and player (b). This happened to me last season in a top football League match when the later cautioned him. The crowd must have been mystified by the booking 4. Have the goal-kick retaken (b). 5. Allow him to take it again (b).

1. John Pickering was sacked last month from the managership of which club?

2. West German internationals Heinz Flohe and Herbert Neumann were in the news while playing for their Bundesliga club Cologne . . . why?

3. Emlyn Hughes was linked recently with which Third Division club in the capacity of player/coach?

4. Name the Doncaster Rovers striker who signed for Aldershot for an estimated £20,000 in mid-May.

5. Watford clinched promotion from the Third Division when they beat Hull City, Chesterfield or Peterborough 2-0, 3-0 or 4-0 at Vicarage Road?

6. Peter Bonetti (below) played against F.A. Cup winners Arsenal at Stamford Bridge on May 14th. What was so significant for the Chelsea goalkeeper in this 1-1 draw?

10. Barcelona played Fortuna Dusseldorf in the Final of the European Cup-Winners' Cup in Basle. Did the Spaniards win 2-1, 3-2 or 4-3?

11. Which two clubs met in the F.A. Youth Cup Final recently?

12. What was the result of the first Scottish Cup Final replay between Rangers and Hibernian?

13. Which talented West Ham midfield player — rated at £200,000 — was recently fined for remarks he made in a national newspaper about the club's policies?

14. Trevor Ross, Bob Latchford or Colin Todd was sent-off while playing for Everton on tour against an Egyptian side.

15. Tommy Docherty is in his second spell as manager of Queens Park Rangers. Did he stay at Loftus Road 18, 28 or 38 days the first time?

7. Can you name the Champions of (a) First, (b) Second, (c) Third and (d) Fourth Divisions?

8. Which Spurs defender broke his right leg in the Republic of Ireland's 1-0 European Championship defeat by Bulgaria in Sofia?

9. Swansea City's Alan Curtis was sold for a Third Division record fee of £400,000. Which First Division club did he join?

ANSWERS

1. Blackburn Rovers. 2. They were both sent-off against Kevin Keegan's side, Hamburger SV. 3. Blackpool. 4. Mick French. 5. Hull City 4-0. 6. It was his 600th — and last — League game for Chelsea. 7. (a) Liverpool, (b) Crystal Palace, (c) Shrewsbury, (d) Reading. 8. Jimmy Holmes. 9. Leeds United 10. 4-3. 11. Manchester City and Millwall. 12. 0-0. 13. Alan Curbishley. 14. Trevor Ross. 15. 28 days.

---

9 JUNE 1979

Who wants to be the man with the whistle?

We all have dreams of scoring a great solo goal, or of making a heroic goal-line clearance. In fact there probably is not one of the 22 players on the park that we wouldn't mind swopping places with. But what about the referee, the man who controls the game?

IF you were asked the question, "What do you think of the average referee?" probably you would instantly reply with Eric and Ernie's well-known comment . . . . RUBBISH!

The players are, of course, the ones you go to see, and it is only natural that they should be the ones to get your praise and admiration. But the poor old referee not only seems to miss out on the glory and hero-worship, he also comes in for much abuse and criticism. Dressed in black he becomes a pantomime demon, who stands for everything evil and bad — the

enemy of the good players.

The referee is always on a hiding to nothing. Every decision he makes is wrong in someone's eyes.

Yet without him there would be no match!

So rather than being the villain of the piece, he is the man who makes the whole thing possible.

Referees handling League matches have the difficult job of controlling 22 professional athletes in a fast moving game in which a great deal can be at stake.

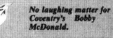

No laughing matter for Coventry's Bobby McDonald.

The action-replays and match reports in the paper act as unofficial judges on his performance, ready to pounce on any controversial incident.

Many believe that referees do a difficult job extremely well. But it is not just the League referee who the crowds love to hate.

The attitude of spectators, and often of players, towards the ref, is less than pleasant in park games, local Leagues and even in school soccer.

Whether it be Wembley or Wimbledon Common the ref still takes all the stick that is flying around.

SHOOT is not saying the ref is perfect, but we are pointing out that players and spectators alike are no nearer to perfection than the man in the middle. After all referees are only human. But what about a bit more tolerance for the ref?

It seems such a shame at schoolboy level to see players arguing with the ref, disputing his decisions and not paying enough attention to playing the game.

Many refs aren't in control of a match just to hear the sound of their own whistle, or for any personal glory. Youth leaders, teachers and parents often go to great lengths and give up a lot of time to see that organised matches can be played. They are putting themselves out so that you lads can enjoy a game of soccer.

Criticise

If you turn out for a side and all the other players do is to criticise your play, call you 'Rubbish', and are openly hostile to you, what would you think? Probably, what's the point of you wasting your time with a load of ungrateful kids who can't get on with the job in hand . . . namely to play, and enjoy, a good game of soccer.

There is no reason why a ref should put up with such similar shoddy treatment!

Next time you go and see your favourite team and the referee gives a decision which you don't agree with, bite your tongue first and think about what he has done.

More often than not you will find the official to have been in the right. If he did make a mistake then at least it shows he is as human as the rest of us!

And when your goal is disallowed, don't waste time and effort bombarding the referee with insults.

Just think to yourself: "Would I like to be doing his job?"

YOU ARE THE REF
Compiled by CLIVE THOMAS

1 A player hurts his arm and takes a throw-in with one hand. Should you:
(a) award a throw-in to the opposition,
(b) take no action, or
(c) make the player retake the throw?

2 After centreing the ball an attacker cannot prevent himself from running over the goal-line. The ball is headed back in his direction by an opponent. The attacker then runs back on the pitch and obtains possession. Should you:
(a) take no action,
(b) stop play and restart by dropping the ball or
(c) caution the attacker?

3 The ball bursts on the top of a halfway flag post. Should you: (a) restart with a throw-in, (b) drop a new ball on the touch-line or (c) drop a new ball where it was last kicked?

4 You are about to drop the ball when you see a defender kick an opponent inside the area. After dismissing the defender should you restart with: (a) a drop ball or (b) a penalty-kick?

5 After a previous warning a player deliberately falls in the penalty-area again and appeals for a penalty. Should you: (a) take no action, (b) warn him again or (c) caution the player?

ANSWERS

1. Award a throw-in to the opposition (a). 2. Take no action (a). 3. Restart with a throw-in (a). 4. A drop ball (a). 5. Caution the player (c). These days players are being called "cheats", because they are taking "dives", or getting other players sent-off unnecessarily. I still believe that it is the referees who should be more professional and catch these players at their own game.

Go for the Double

After solving the clues in this specially compiled crossword, you can use the letters in the thick-edged squares to form the name of an Arsenal defender. Answers on page 46.

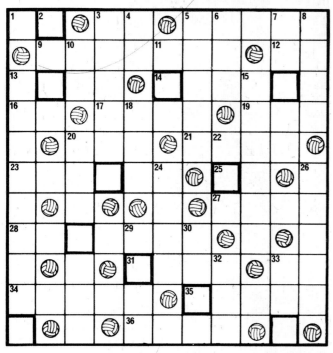

ACROSS:—
(1) Paul Br--h of West Ham
(3) — Ahead Eagles; Dutch League club.
(5) Body part which needs to be kept slim.
(9) Many goals result from them.
(12) The P--ters (Stoke City). The missing letters reversed.
(13) Dennis —, Leicester City defender.
(14) Arnold —, Ipswich Town midfield player.
(16) Luton Town, The H--ters.
(17) Turned round and round.
(19) Le--ash-n (1963 European Footballer of the Year). Plant from the omissions.
(20) Bri--ol Cit-, Division One club.
(21) Ha-- A--nue (Southport). Donate from the missing letters.
(23) A French League club.
(25) Rene Hous--an (Argentine star). The omissions reversed.
(27) -o-tman R-a-; Ipswich Town's ground.
(28) Scottish club who won everything they played for in 1929/30, 1933/34 and 1977/78.
(31) ---tton P-rk (Portsmouth). A distant word from the missing letters.
(33) S--rtak Trnava; European club.
(34) A surprise result, for instance.
(35) — Road, ground of Colchester
(36) One of four allowed to the goalkeeper whilst holding the ball.

DOWN:—
(2) Frank Gray (Nottingham Forest) is one.
(3) — Road, Crewe Alexandra.
(4) Millwall, The Li--s.
(5) Twisted.
(6) -lder--ot from the Recreation Ground.
(7) — Coppell of Manchester United.
(8) — Sealey of Crystal Palace.
(10) Queen -- the South, Scottish club.
(11) G-rd--ller; famous European player.
(13) Expressing ecstatic delight.
(15) Gianni —, European Footballer of the Year, 1969.
(18) Jesse —, former famous name with Luton Town.
(20) Graeme —, Liverpool midfield player.
(22) Lincoln City are nicknamed The ---s.
(24) H-dde---ield Town. "Foam" from the missing letters.
(26) — Street, ground of Hereford United.
(29) Consumes food from one's seats!
(30) Take four letters from Newcastle for an auction.
(32) Smart slight blow.
(33) -r--ton Park, Tranmere Rovers.

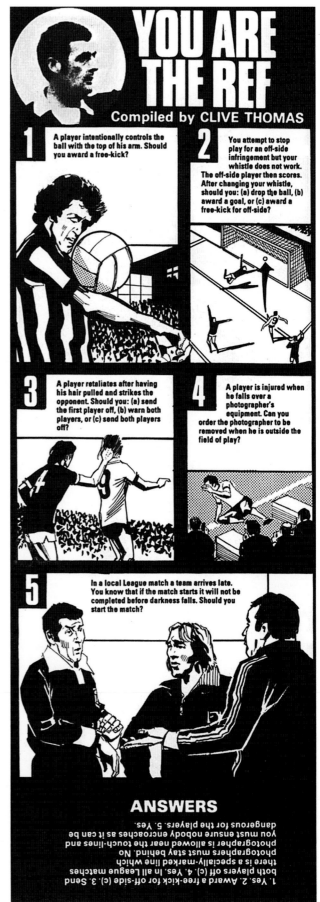

YOU ARE THE REF

Compiled by CLIVE THOMAS

1 A player intentionally controls the ball with the top of his arm. Should you award a free-kick?

2 You attempt to stop play for an off-side infringement but your whistle does not work. The off-side player then scores. After changing your whistle, should you: (a) drop the ball, (b) award a goal, or (c) award a free-kick for off-side?

3 A player retaliates after having his hair pulled and strikes the opponent. Should you: (a) send the first player off, (b) warn both players, or (c) send both players off?

4 A player is injured when he falls over a photographer's equipment. Can you order the photographer to be removed when he is outside the field of play?

5 In a local League match a team arrives late. You know that if the match starts it will not be completed before darkness falls. Should you start the match?

ANSWERS

1. Yes. 2. Award a free-kick for off-side (c). 3. Send both players off (c). 4. Yes. In all League matches there is a specially-marked line behind which photographers must stay behind. No photographer is allowed near the touch-lines and you must ensure nobody encroaches as it can be dangerous for the players. 5. Yes.

YOU ARE THE REF

Compiled by CLIVE THOMAS

1 Before a penalty-kick is taken a defender obtains your permission to leave the pitch. The defender stands near a goal post. Can you order him to move in case he distracts the penalty-taker?

2 Taking a corner, a player miskicks the ball. The goalkeeper runs outside the area kicks the ball into his penalty-area, picks it up and clears down the field. Should you (a) have the kick retaken or (b) take no action?

3 Can a goalkeeper wear number 21 on his back?

4 A defending player obstructs an opponent and pushes him at the same time. Should you award (a) a direct free-kick or (b) indirect free-kick?

5 A free-kick is awarded to the attacking side. You are assuring the defenders are ten yards from the ball when an attacking player shoots wide. Should you (a) have the kick retaken or (b) take no action?

ANSWERS

1. Yes. 2. Take no action (b). 3. Yes. 4. Direct free-kick (a). 5. Take no action (b). It happened in my game at Highbury in the local derby between Arsenal and Tottenham. I had given a free-kick to Tottenham just outside the Arsenal penalty-area. After placing the ball I went forward to mark the ten yards when Yorath took the kick. His shot went wide and I restarted with a goal-kick. Brian Talbot asked me what would I have given if the ball had gone into the goal. I said "I would have made them retake the kick."

4 OCTOBER 1980

YOU ARE THE REF

Compiled by CLIVE THOMAS

1 A goalkeeper clears the ball, but also trips an attacker inside the penalty-area. The attacker falls outside the area. Should you (a) take no action, (b) award a penalty, or (c) a direct free-kick outside the penalty-area?

2 Can you signal a player who has received treatment back on the field without stopping play?

3 A captain, wearing an armband, questions your decision. Should you (a) take no action, (b) listen to the player's comments or (c) caution him?

4 After tossing a coin, the losing captain claims the right to decide the kick-off because in error you allowed the visitors skipper to call. Do you (a) let the decision stand or (b) toss the coin again?

5 Immediately after awarding a goal you realise the ball did not cross the goal-line. Should you (a) stick to your goal decision, (b) drop the ball where you stopped play, or (c) award a goal-kick?

ANSWERS

1. Award a penalty (b). 2. Yes. 3. Caution the player (c). Although in British football the captains do not wear armbands, in Europe they are always used. Unfortunately these players then seem to think they have a right to question decisions and commit offences. I was refereeing Bayern Munich and Real Madrid in the European Cup Semi-Final second-leg in Munich and had already cautioned the Real Madrid captain during the first-half. Then with 30 seconds to go to the end of the game he continued to question a decision I made. I then sent him off. I understand he never played for Real again. 4. Let the decision stand (a). 5. Drop the ball where you stopped play (b).

27 DECEMBER 1980

YOU ARE THE REF

compiled by Keith Hackett

1 At half-time your linesman informs you he will be unable to resume in the second-half due to injury. Should you abandon the match?

2 A forward with the ball is stopped by a defender who grabs his shirt. Should you: (a) Stop play and award a direct free-kick, or (b) wave play on?

3 You blow your whistle to stop play because a forward is in an offside position. The forward picks up the ball and brings it to you applauding your decision. Should you: (a) Caution him, or (b) take no action?

MATCH POINT

● One disturbing infringement I've noticed as a result of the three points for a win system is the increase in the number of goalkeepers wasting time. Many seem to think that as long as they don't take more than four steps, they can hang on to the ball all day. I haven't had to take any direct action so far, but I can see that refs will have to start awarding indirect free-kicks, and even cautioning 'keepers, if they don't speed things up. And talking about the four steps rule, many 'keepers don't realise that it's not enough to just bounce the ball after taking four paces and then taking another few. I just carry on counting until the 'keeper has clearly released the ball to another player. Once again an indirect free-kick is the punishment. So watch out you 'keepers — you have been warned!

ANSWERS

1. No. You would ask the home club officials to make an announcement over the public address system asking for a replacement. Some clubs in the Football League do have a stand-by official from the local area available. For the F.A. Cup Final I had a reserve linesman standing by in case. 2. The player is guilty of an act of ungentlemanly conduct, and should also be cautioned (a) 3. By picking up the ball and bringing it to you applauding at the same time, the player is clearly guilty of showing dissent by his actions against your decision (a) Players must refrain from disputing referees' decisions.

YOU ARE THE REF

compiled by Keith Hackett

1 At the taking of a penalty the ball strikes a post and bursts? Do you (a) award a goal, (b) have the kick retaken or (c) drop the ball to restart the game?

2 Having asked your permission to have an injury attended to, a player receives the ball as he is leaving the field and scores. Do you (a) award a goal (b) send the player off and disallow the goal or (c) caution the player?

3 A defender strikes an opponent whilst in the penalty-area. The ball is in play. Do you (a) send the player off and award a penalty kick or (b) warn the player and restart the game with a drop ball?

MATCH POINT

● Recent weather conditions have certainly made my job a lot tougher. The European tie between Floriana and Standard Liege in Malta was played in high humidity, on a very hard pitch of clay and sand with a temperature of some 85 degrees. But three days later I was at Blackburn for the game against Leicester and it absolutely poured. In the first game physical contact was almost impossible, and many players were very visibly shocked after taking a tumble on the rock hard ground. At Blackburn there was a lot of surface water and the ball was sticking in puddles. In both cases I had to make allowances for things which often I wouldn't have let go. But it had to work both ways, and I'm pleased to report that the players respected and appreciated what I was trying to do and kept within the laws and spirit of the game.

ANSWERS

1. C. But if the ball burst whilst the game was added on at the end of the game for the taking of the penalty kick the game would end immediately the ball hit the post and burst. 2. C. You would restart the game by awarding an indirect free-kick to his opponents team at the point where he kicked the ball. 3. A. Players who strike opponents, kick and spit do the game a great disservice. They deserve to be sent-off.

Meet the REAL cloggers

"THE REAL hatchetmen are not the recognised hard players—Harris, Storey, Norman Hunter. They're hard all right, but they're fair and not cowards.

"The real cloggers work on the referee's blind side and under the cover of other players—players whose sole job is to con the ref into looking the other way."

—ALLAN CLARKE, Leeds.

CLARKE

THE LAW MAN
Watch for the 'law man' who jumps between two opponents about to throw punches. He's conned the ref into thinking he's cooled the situation, but look down at his feet. You'll see he's crunching hell out of the ENEMY'S feet.

THE BOY SCOUT
Watch for the visiting player who retrieves the ball for the home side. This act—which both crowd and ref love—is usually a blind to draw attention from another corner of the field where one of his mates is busy clobbering an opponent.

STOREY

LAUGHING BOY
He takes a tumble with an opponent — appeals, gets turned down and acknowledges it all with a laugh. Another tumble — another con attempt — and another big grin. The ref's not amused, he looks the other way — a big mistake for it gives laughing boy his chance to put the boot in for real.

THE NIGGLER
This merchant would top every good conduct league. He never questions a decision or shows resentment. But once he gets on the referee's blind side, the knife's out. He niggles at players with fiery temperaments, taunting them and kicking them when their backs are turned.

DECOY DUCK
Just before a corner is taken he darts into what appears to be a better scoring position. He's ensured he's right under the ref's nose when he fakes a whack from behind. The ref, not sure what's happening, keeps his eye on the situation and misses the real clogging behind.

HARRIS

DEVISED AND DRAWN BY TREVILLION

YOU ARE THE REF
compiled by Keith Hackett

1 A defender miskicks a goal-kick, which only just travels outside the penalty-area. He follows the ball up and kicks it for a second time. Should you:
(a) wave play on, or (b) award an indirect free kick?

2 With time running out a goalkeeper is injured and has to be substituted. His team decide to play on without anybody in goal. Is this permissible?

3 You see an offence taking place, but wave play on. The advantage, however, does not materialise and the player loses possession. Should you:
(a) allow play to continue, or (b) stop play and award a free-kick for the offence?

PLAY ON

MATCH POINT

THE question of dissent is one of the greatest problems facing a modern day ref, and one must question what players are hoping to achieve by disputing the referee's decisions. It is very rare that a ref is going to change his decision when a player shows dissention, and so it really is a pointless show of petulance. Often I find that captains believe that they have a right to question your decisions on behalf of team-mates, but they run just as much chance of being booked. You often find yourself keeping a closer eye on a player who continually disputes your decisions, because a player who can't control his mouth often can't control his feet either.

ANSWERS

1. Award an indirect free-kick (b). 2. No. The law states clearly that one member of the team must be a goalkeeper. 3. Allow play to continue by taking no action (a). Most experienced referees strive to make full use of the advantage clause. The occasional advantage does not always work out, but referees have to make accurate and quick judgments when and when not to allow play to continue. The more experienced referees strive to make full use of the advantage clause. The occasional advantage whenever possible, providing the players are responding to the ref's actions and not escalating the offences.

HUG—AND A BOOKING

UNUSUAL incident in the Spanish Cup match between Tarragona and Badalona.

The visitors were awarded a penalty in the 42nd minute, but Rebollo blasted it high and wide. Tarragona defender Santiago was so pleased that he gave Rebollo a hug . . . and the referee promptly awarded a second penalty for ungentlemanly conduct.

Rebollo tried again with the spot kick, and missed again.

This time Santiago kept his feelings under control!

PRICEY SOCCER

A RECENT survey of entrance fees in Spain makes interesting reading at a time when many British fans are complaining about high prices. Just take a look at this table of terrace and main stand prices in Spain's premier First Division stadiums:

Club	Terraces	Main Stand (seats)
Ath. Bilbao	£1.80	£7.80
At. Madrid	£3.00	£7.80
Barcelona	£4.80	£10.80
Español	£3.60	£9.50
Gijon	£3.60	£9.50
Hercules	£3.60	£9.50
Real Sociedad	£2.95	£9.00
Real Madrid	£2.40	£7.75
Sevilla	£4.80	£8.75
Valencia	£2.95	£9.00
Zaragoza	£3.60	£9.00

In most cases these figures are almost doubled for attractive games against the likes of Real Madrid, and for all European games!
● Photo shows the San Mames Stadium, Bilbao.

● Hamburger SV star Franz Beckenbauer (left) is finding what life is like on the other side of the fence as a radio reporter.

YOU ARE THE REF

compiled by Keith Hackett

1 A team in the process of taking five penalty-kicks to decide the winner of a Cup competition change the goalkeeper. An outfield player takes his place. Do you (a) allow the game to continue, allowing the change to take place or (b) refuse permission?

2 A throws to B then runs from the touchline to position A2. B passes the ball back to A in position A2 who then goes through and scores. Do you (a) allow the goal or (b) award an indirect free-kick for offside?

3 When the ball is on the halfway line, you notice the goalkeeper strike a forward in the penalty-area. Do you (a) award a penalty and send the goalkeeper off or (b) stop play, caution the 'keeper and restart the game with a drop ball?

MATCH POINT

The recent bad weather has made my job particularly difficult. When deciding whether a game can be played, your first priority must be player safety. You must also try to get an accurate weather forecast, because there is no use in starting a match if it is going to be turned into a farce by deteriorating conditions. And you must always consider the fans. A game cannot be played if the terraces are dangerous or if the exits from the ground are blocked. I postponed the Nottingham Forest v Ipswich game two days in advance because there was no way the pitch was going to get any better in those 48 hours, and I didn't want Ipswich or their fans to have a long journey in vain.

ANSWERS:

1. Allow the change to take place (a). The team, however, must inform you that they intend making a change. 2. Award an indirect free-kick for offside when the ball was passed from B to A2. 3. Award a penalty and send the goalkeeper off (a). Your linesmen have a duty to watch for off the ball offences. Players are not going to get away with this type of serious offence if committed behind the referee's back.

LINE-UPS... RESU

Saturday, Dec 5
(Continued)

Scottish Premier

MORTON (0) 2 (McNeil, Houston)
ABERDEEN (0) 1 (Hewitt)　3,200
Morton: Baines, Hayes, Holmes, McLaughlin, Orr, Rooney, Busby, Docherty, McNeil, Hutchison, Houston.
Aberdeen: Leighton, Kennedy, McMaster (Cooper), Simpson, McLeish, Miller, Strachan, Watson, McGhee (Hewitt), Black, Weir.

ST MIRREN (0) 2 (Bone, Stark)
PARTICK (0) 1 (Park)　4,513
St Mirren: Thomson, McCormack, Beckett (Logan), Fulton, Copland, Fitzpatrick, Stark, Abercrombie, McAvennie, Somner (Bone), Scanlon.
Partick: Rough, Murray, Whittaker, Dunlop, Anderson, Jardine, Doyle, Park, Watson, Johnston, Higgins.

Scottish First

AYR (0) 2 (Morris 2)
RAITH (0) 0　780

CLYDEBANK (1) 2 (Millar, Coyne)
QoS (0) 1 (McCann)　400

DUNFERMLINE (1) 1 (McNaughton pen)
KILMARNOCK (2) 2 (McBride, McDicken)　2,000

EAST STIRLING (0) 0
MOTHERWELL (2) 6 (Carson, Forbes, Rafferty, Irvine, McLelland, McLaughlin pen)　970

HAMILTON (2) 2 (Brown, McDowell)
FALKIRK (0) 0　1,000

HEARTS (0) 1 (Pettigrew)
QUEEN'S PARK (0) 1 (McNiven pen)　3,971

ST JOHNSTONE (2) 5 (Weir 2, Morton, Mackay, Brogan)
DUMBARTON (1) 2 (Blair, Kenny pen)　1,776

Scottish Second

ARBROATH (0) 2 (Gavine, Yule)
ALLOA (1) 1 (McComb)　560

BERWICK (3) 6 (Lawson 3, Davidson, McCulloch, McGlynn)
ALBION (1) 1 (Burgess)　745

EAST FIFE (1) 2 (Caithness, Scott)
BRECHIN (0) 2 (Mackie, Henderson)　531

MEADOWBANK (1) 2 (Sproat, Godfrey)
CLYDE (2) 3 (Dempsey, Nevin, Hood)　350

MONTROSE (1) 2 (Campbell, Fletcher)
COWDENBEATH (1) 2 (Forrest pen, McFarland)　300

STIRLING (1) 2 (Kennedy, McNeil)
STENHOUSEMUIR (1) 3 (Murray 2, Jenkins pen)　460

STRANRAER (0) 2 (Sweeney, Murphy)
FORFAR (0) 1 (McPhee)　506

Tuesday, Dec 8

First Division

SOUTHAMPTON (0) 0
BRIGHTON (0) 2 (Ritchie, Gatting)　22,128
Southampton: Katalinic, Golac, Holmes, Williams, Nicholl, Waldron, Keegan, Channon, Moran, Armstrong, Ball.
Brighton: Moseley, Shanks, Nelson, Grealish, Foster, Gatting, Ryan, Smith, Ritchie, McNab, Thomas.

Football League Cup

(Fourth Round replay)

LIVERPOOL (0) 3 (Johnston, McDermott pen, Dalglish)
ARSENAL (0) 0　AET 21,375
Liverpool: Grobbelaar, Neal, Lawrenson, Kennedy (A), Kennedy (R), Hansen, Dalglish, Lee, Rush, McDermott, Souness.
Arsenal: Wood, Robson, Sansom, Talbot, O'Leary, Whyte, Hollins, Sunderland, Davis, Nicholas (Hankin), Rix.

Postponed Crystal Palace v WBA.

Group Cup

(Quarter Finals)

BURNLEY (2) 2 (Scott, Holt)
WATFORD (0) 1 (Blissett)　2,658

NEWPORT (0) 0
GRIMSBY (1) 2 (Beacock, Drinkell)　2,206

Wednesday, Dec 9

U.E.F.A. CUP

(Third Round, second leg)

DUNDEE UTD (3) 5 (Bannon, Narey, Hegarty, Milne 2)
WINTERSLAG (0) 0　16,232
Dundee Utd: McAlpine, Holt, Malpas, Phillip, Hegarty, Narey, Bannon, Milne, Kirkwood, Sturrock, Dodds.
(Dundee Utd win 5-0 on agg.)

HAMBURGER SV (1) 3 (Hrubesch, Memering pen, Jakobs)
ABERDEEN (0) 1 (McGhee)　45,600
Aberdeen: Leighton, Kennedy, McMaster, Watson, McLeish, Miller, Strachan (McGhee), Cooper, Black, Simpson, Hewitt.
(Hamburger SV win 5-4 on agg.)

Football League Cup

(Fourth Round)

Postponed: Crystal Palace v WBA; Everton v Ipswich.

Group Cup

(Quarter Final)

BRADFORD (1) 1 (Jackson)
SHREWSBURY (0) 1 (Dungworth)　2,144
(AET Shrewsbury win 4-3 on penalties)

Saturday, Dec 12

First Division

COVENTRY (0) 0
MANCHESTER CITY (1) 1 (Tueart)　12,398
Coventry: Blyth, Thomas, Roberts (Kaiser), Jacobs, Dyson, Gillespie, Hendrie, Daly, Thompson, Hateley, Hunt.
Man City: Corrigan, Ranson, McDonald, Reid, Bond, Caton, Tueart, Reeves, Francis, Hartford, Hutchison.

LEEDS 0
TOTTENHAM 0　28,780
Leeds: Lukic, Cherry, Gray (F), Stevenson, Hart, Burns, Harris, Graham, Butterworth (Connor), Hamson, Hird.
Tottenham: Clemence, Hughton, Miller, Roberts, Hazard (Lacy), Perryman, Ardiles, Villa, Galvin, Hoddle, Crooks.

Brighton's Andy Ritchie.

Ask THE Expert

Send your letters to: Ask the Expert, SHOOT!, King's Reach Tower, Stamford Street, London SE1 9LS. U.K. readers receive £2 for every letter published. Overseas readers receive a special SHOOT T-shirt. When writing, please state size: small, medium or large. While every letter is read, our Expert regrets he cannot reply to individual letters personally.

FIFA Firsts

When was FIFA founded, who were the first members, and how many are there now?

OLIVER NWACHUKWU,
NIGERIA

● FIFA (Federation of International Football Associations) was founded in Paris on 21st May, 1904, Oliver, by the national Football Associations of France, Belgium, Denmark, Holland, Spain, Sweden, and Switzerland. There are now, at the latest count, 152 member-nations.

Pele's goals

When, and against whom, did Pele score his first, 100th, 500th, and 1,000th first-class goal?

MOSES SEFA,
GHANA

● All were scored for Santos, Moses — the first being against Corinthians on 7th September, 1956.
The hundredth came against Commercial on 31st July, 1958; and the five hundredth against Botafogo on 5th September, 1962.
Pele hit home number 1,000 from the penalty-spot against Vasco de Gama on 18th November, 1969.

Dutch drama

What was the quickest penalty ever awarded in a major international Cup Final?

CHRIS SPRAY,
NEW ZEALAND

● Shouldn't think one's come much quicker than that which English referee Jack Taylor gave in the 1974 World Cup Final in Munich, Chris.
Not a single West German player had touched the ball between the Dutch kick-off and the moment that Johan Cruyff, spurting into the penalty-area, was brought down by Uli Hoeness.
The home fans were shocked into stunned silence as Johan Neeskens coolly sent 'keeper Sepp Maier the wrong way to give Holland the lead — later wiped out by Paul Breitner (another penalty) and Gerd Muller to make the Cup safe for West Germany.

Sir Stanley Matthews

When did the great Sir Stanley Matthews play his first, and last, League match?

NICHOLAS CURTIS,
WISBECH

● His first League game for Stoke, Nicholas, was in March, 1932 at the age of just 17.
His last, also for Stoke, was at Fulham on 6th February, 1965 — five days after his 50th birthday. That was Sir Stan's 701st peacetime League game — a total which, but for the long Wartime break in normal football, would have been pushing the thousand mark.

Stanley Matthews

Spot-on Lee

Who's scored the most Football League penalties in a season?

PAUL BRANDRETT,
HARPENDEN

● 27-cap former England star Francis Lee holds that record, Paul. He scored 13 times from the spot for Manchester City in the First Division in 1971-72 — plus another one apiece in both the F.A. Cup and League Cup.

SHORT PASSES

● Liverpool have played in one or other of the "Big Three" Euro competitions every season since 1964-65.

(PIOTR DEREZINSKI, Poland)

● Record F.A. Cup Final victory is Bury 6, Derby County 0 (1903); followed by Blackburn Rovers 6, Sheffield Wednesday 1 (1890).

(ALISTAIR SMITH, Carlisle)

● Record Fourth Division gate is 37,774 (Palace v. Millwall; 31st March, 1961).

(RICHARD McGEOUGH, Basingstoke)

Short Passes are replies to readers' letters.

Johan Neeskens scores from the penalty spot for Holland against West Germany in the early stages of the 1974 World Cup Final.

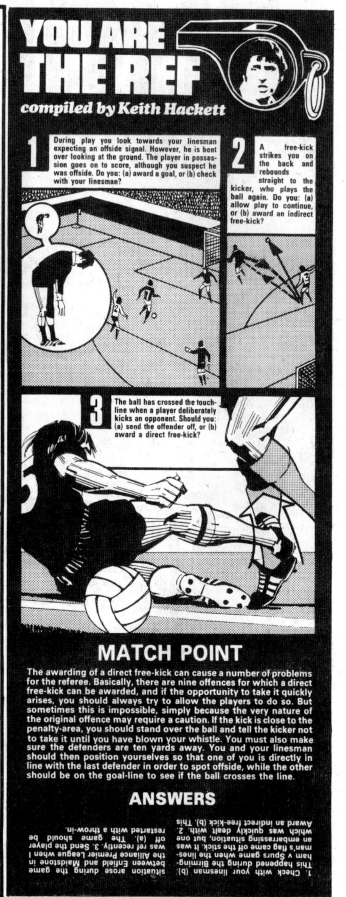

YOU ARE THE REF

compiled by Keith Hackett

1 During play you look towards your linesman expecting an offside signal. However, he is bent over looking at the ground. The player in possession goes on to score, although you suspect he was offside. Do you: (a) award a goal, or (b) check with your linesman?

2 A free-kick strikes you on the back and rebounds straight to the kicker, who plays the ball again. Do you: (a) allow play to continue, or (b) award an indirect free-kick?

3 The ball has crossed the touch-line when a player deliberately kicks an opponent. Should you: (a) send the offender off, or (b) award a direct free-kick?

MATCH POINT

The awarding of a direct free-kick can cause a number of problems for the referee. Basically, there are nine offences for which a direct free-kick can be awarded, and if the opportunity to take it quickly arises, you should always try to allow the players to do so. But sometimes this is impossible, simply because the very nature of the original offence may require a caution. If the kick is close to the penalty-area, you should stand over the ball and tell the kicker not to take it until you have blown your whistle. You must also make sure the defenders are ten yards away. You and your linesman should then position yourselves so that one of you is directly in line with the last defender in order to spot offside, while the other should be on the goal-line to see if the ball crosses the line.

ANSWERS

1. Check with your linesman (b). This happened during the Birmingham v Spurs game when the linesman's flag came off the stick. It was an embarrassing situation, but one which was quickly dealt with. 2. Award an indirect free-kick (b). This situation arose during the game between Enfield and Maidstone in the Alliance Premier League when I was ref recently. 3. Send the player off (a). The game should be restarted with a throw-in.

WHISTLE STOP
Compiled by KEITH HACKETT

Keith kicks off his column with a look at the changes to the Laws.

1 The 'Professional Foul' Any player who deliberately prevents a goal scoring opportunity by foul play shall be considered guilty of serious foul play and should be sent-off by the referee.

2 'Stealing' ground at throw-ins. If a player attempts to take a throw at a different spot to where the ball actually crossed the line, a foul throw shall be awarded.

3 The four-steps rule. The goalkeeper no longer has to be holding the ball to break the four-steps ruling. As soon as the ball is under his control, the four steps begins.

1. If, in the referee's opinion, a goalscoring opportunity has been taken away by means of foul play, then the offender should be sent-off. A player bringing down an opponent who has only the 'keeper to beat should be sent-off. So should a 'keeper who handles outside his area to prevent an opponent reaching the ball. And, the most clear-cut case of all, a player who handles to prevent a goal being scored.

2. In the past, players deliberately took a throw from the wrong place to waste time. Now a ref should indicate where a throw should be taken from, and if the player does not follow his orders a foul throw should be given.

3. Goalkeepers are now either booting the ball wildly upfield or rolling it quickly out to a defender, who messes about with the ball instead, but either way I think it is an amendment which speeds the game up.

TOP:
18 SEPTEMBER 1982

CENTRE:
25 SEPTEMBER 1982

BOTTOM:
16 APRIL 1983

WHISTLE STOP
Compiled by KEITH HACKETT

1 A player brings an opponent down by 'stooping in front of him as the ball is dropping from a goal-kick. Should you award a direct or indirect free-kick?

2 A defender stands six yards away from the ball at a corner kick. Do you allow this?

3 At the start of the game you notice a player in the opponent's half before the game has kicked-off. Should you allow play to proceed?

ANSWERS

1. A direct free-kick. This is an offence which referees should be particularly watchful for. Both defenders and attackers are often guilty of 'making a back' for opponents. 2. No. At the taking of any form of free-kick no opponent must be standing within ten yards of the ball. 3. No, order the player into his own half. It is important for the referee to show he is in control right from the start. Players must stand in their own half at kick-off and the defending side must stand ten yards away. That is why the centre circle is so clearly marked.

WHISTLE STOP
Compiled by KEITH HACKETT

1 The ball has crossed the touchline when a player deliberately hits an opponent. Should you (a) send the offender off, or (b) award a direct free-kick?

2 A player taking a corner, kicks the ball against the corner flag and proceeds to run at goal with the ball. Do you (a) allow play to continue, (b) award a drop ball, or (c) award an in direct free-kick?

3 A defender, seeing a linesman's flag raised, catches the ball. You are satisfied the linesman was incorrect to flag. Do you (a) award a free-kick against the defender, (b) award a drop ball, or (c) play on?

MATCH POINT
I recently had the difficult decision of postponing Oldham's home game with Burnley. Luckily enough, secretary Tom Finn gave me ample warning that the pitch was very heavy. I went to Boundary Park at about 2 o'clock and after checking the weather forecast decided that I could save the Burnley supporters from travelling by calling the game off.

ANSWERS
1. Send the offender off (a). The game should restart with a throw-in. 2. Award an indirect free-kick (c). 3. Award a free-kick against the defender (a).

YOU ARE THE REF

The Observer
2006 -

1

During a penalty shootout you tell the keeper to stay on his line: he responds with a torrent of foul and abusive language, so you send him off. His captain then tells you that, as normal playing time is over, the keeper will be replaced by a nominated substitute. What action, if any, do you take?

ANSWER The captain is wrong: the goalkeeper may only be replaced by an outfield player who was on the field of play at the start of the penalty shootout.

2 A 5ft 2in defender is waiting for an opposition corner to be delivered. With his back to to the corner-taker, the defender jockeys for position and holds out his arms to look bigger. At that moment the kick is taken hard and fast, and strikes the back of his hand. What is your decision?

3 It's raining heavily when you award an indirect free-kick to the defending team. The defender takes it quickly and kicks the ball back to his keeper, who slips on the wet grass and misses it. The ball enters the goal. What do you do?

ANSWER Award a penalty kick: there is no such thing as 'ball to arm' in this situation: the player must take the consequences of his actions. You must also decide whether to caution the player for unsporting behaviour, or, if a goalscoring chance was clearly denied, you must send the player off.

ANSWER Award a corner. You cannot turn an advantage (the free-kick) to your team into a disadvantage by scoring directly against your own side.

1 A player decides to change places with the goalkeeper without informing you before the change is made. What action do you take?

2 As play continues, a player asks if he can leave the field for an urgent toilet break but, as he is jogging off, the ball comes to him, he scores and wheels away to celebrate. What action do you take?

1 You notice that a player whom you sent off earlier for violent conduct has returned in his suit to sit on the bench to watch the remainder of the match. What action do you take?

ANSWERS

1) Wait for the next break in play, and approach the technical area to demand the player is removed. A player who has been sent off must leave the vicinity of the field of play, which includes the technical area.

2) Disallow the goal. It is an offence to prevent a goalkeeper releasing the ball from his hands; the releasing of the ball from his hands and the kicking of the ball are considered to be a single action.

3) Reverse your decision: disallow the goal, send off the goalkeeper for violent conduct and award a penalty to the opposing team.

3 A supporter blows a whistle in the crowd. A defender inside his own area picks the ball up, assuming that play has been stopped by the referee. Opponents bay for a penalty. What action do you take?

ANSWERS
1) Allow play to continue. When the ball is next out of play, call the two players to you and show both the yellow card for breaking Law 3, requiring any goalkeeper change to be overseen by the referee.
2) Disallow the goal and caution the player for unsporting behaviour. The game is restarted with an indirect free-kick, taken from the place where the infringement occurred.
3) Stop play because of 'outside interference' and restart the match with a dropped ball from the place where the player picked the ball up. You should also liaise with security officers to ask that they apprehend the culprit.

2 A goalkeeper prepares to kick upfield – but a small attacker appears from behind him, intercepts the ball before it hits the ground and scores. What do you do?

3 A goal is scored. You give it, but then notice a signal from your assistant at the other end of the field. The assistant tells you that as the ball was entering the goal, the goalkeeper at the other end punched an opponent inside his own penalty area. What action do you take?

1 A midfielder develops a nosebleed, which he is mopping up with his shirt. At the next stoppage, you call on the physio who insists the bleed is nothing serious and that the player can play on, with a tissue. What is your reply?

2 You whistle for half time. On leaving the field you glance at your watches again and realise to your embarrassment that you've played for only 42 minutes. Do you play 48 minutes in the second half to compensate, or 42 to make both halves equal?

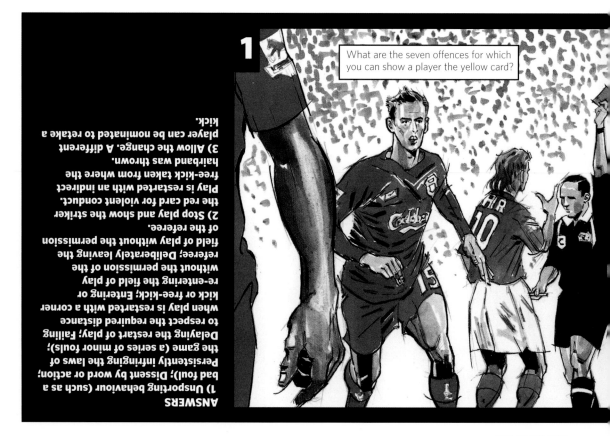

1 What are the seven offences for which you can show a player the yellow card?

ANSWERS
1) Unsporting behaviour (such as a bad foul); Dissent by word or action; Persistently infringing the laws of the game (a series of minor fouls); Delaying the restart of play; Failing to respect the required distance when play is restarted with a corner kick or free-kick; Entering or re-entering the field of play without the permission of the referee; Deliberately leaving the field of play without the permission of the referee.
2) Stop play and show the striker the red card for violent conduct. Play is restarted with an indirect free-kick taken from where the hairband was thrown. 3) Allow the change. A different player can be nominated to retake a kick.

3 Towards the end of the first half in a Conference game, you are increasingly concerned that one of your assistants – an inexperienced official – is making wrong, nervous decisions, and failing in his duties. Both managers demand you 'get rid' of him. What action do you take, if any?

ANSWERS

1) You must remove the player from the field and do not allow him back until the bleeding has stopped. He must also change his shirt if it is contaminated with blood: all Premiership clubs have back-up plain shirts, without name or number.

2) Neither. You must bring the players back on to the field and play the remaining three minutes of the first half. Half time is then taken, followed by a normal 45-minute second half.

3) If you decide the assistant's performance constitutes undue interference or improper conduct, you can relieve him of his duties and call on the fourth official. But this is extremely unlikely to happen above grassroots level: selection procedures for promotion to the **senior level of the game are stringent.**

2 A striker loses his cool with a substitute from his own side who is standing in the technical area. The substitute has been goading him for missing a string of chances: the striker snaps and throws his hairband, hitting the substitute in the face. What action do you take?

3 A goalkeeper saves a penalty kick but was off his line – you order it to be retaken. The original nominated kicker, though, has lost his self-belief and asks a team-mate to retake the kick. What action do you take?

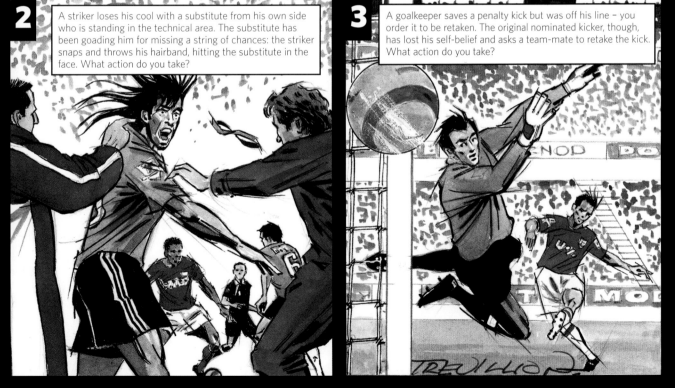

1 In the last minute of a Champions League tie a defender boots the ball into the stands to waste time. An opposition player grabs a ball from a ballboy and throws it to his team-mate, who takes a first-time shot. After the shot is struck but before it enters the net, the original ball is thrown down from the crowd and enters the field of play. What action do you take?

2 A player taking a penalty kick steps over the ball and backheels it to a team-mate, who hammers it into the net past a bewildered goalkeeper, striking the ball just before it travels outside the penalty area. What action do you take?

1 You make a controversial decision while refereeing an Under-11s match. A furious father on the touchline embarks on a continuous torrent of foul verbal abuse against you. What action, if any, do you take?

ANSWERS 1) Stop play and request the presence of a home club official. Remind the official that the club is responsible for the conduct of spectators; tell them to deal with the father, and advise them you will be reporting the matter to the relevant authorities. If the club fails to deal with the father, you must abandon the game. The FA's Child Protection Policy covers not only officials and coaches, but also the behaviour of those watching. **2)** You cannot intervene at this stage. Allow the match to proceed and report the facts to the Premier League at the end of the game. **3)** At the next stoppage in play, advise your colleagues to observe the players while you leave the field for a comfort break. Restart play as normal when you return.

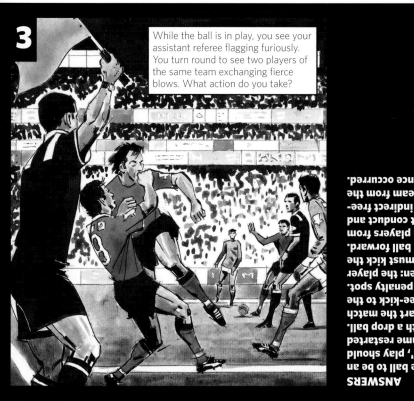

3

While the ball is in play, you see your assistant referee flagging furiously. You turn round to see two players of the same team exchanging fierce blows. What action do you take?

ANSWERS
1) If you consider the ball to be an 'outside interference', play should be stopped and the game restarted with a drop ball.
2) Stop play and restart the match with an indirect free-kick to the defending team on the penalty spot. Law 14 has been broken: the player taking the penalty must kick the ball forward.
3) Stop play, send both players from the field for violent conduct and restart play with an indirect free-kick to the opposing team from the place where the offence occurred.

2

It's a baking hot day. As you prepare to start the second half, the fourth official informs you that the pitch was watered during half time – but only the end that the home team are attacking. What action do you take?

3

At half time you drank a lot of water. There are 10 minutes to go and you are now desperate to use the toilet. You risk embarassing yourself on live television. What do you do?

TREVILLION

1

A player takes a penalty kick and sends the goalkeeper the wrong way. However, as he is about to celebrate, a dog runs on to the field and nods the ball to safety. What action do you take?

2

A penalty strikes the post and rebounds straight to the penalty taker. With the keeper on his back, the penalty taker prepares to slot home the rebound – but as he lines up his shot, he's brought down in the box by a defender. What is your decision?

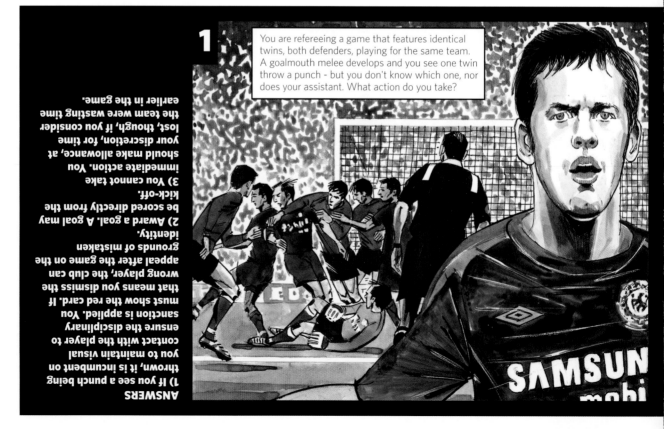

1

You are refereeing a game that features identical twins, both defenders, playing for the same team. A goalmouth melee develops and you see one twin throw a punch - but you don't know which one, nor does your assistant. What action do you take?

ANSWERS
1) If you see a punch being thrown, it is incumbent on you to maintain visual contact with the player to ensure the disciplinary sanction is applied. You must show the red card. If that means you dismiss the wrong player, the club can appeal after the game on the grounds of mistaken identity.
2) Award a goal. A goal may be scored directly from the kick-off.
3) You cannot take immediate action. You should make allowance, at your discretion, for time lost, though, if you consider the team were wasting time earlier in the game.

3 A player is substituted and leaves the field of play. You signal to allow his replacement on to the field. The sub acknowledges your signal, but before entering the field takes a throw-in. What action do you take, if any?

ANSWERS
1) Award a drop ball at the point where the dog - an 'outside interference' - intervened. If, as in this case, the incident occurred inside the goal area, the drop ball takes place on the goal area line (parallel to the goalline) at the point nearest to where the ball was when play was stopped. **2) Award another penalty, but do not send the defender off.** This was not an obvious goalscoring opportunity, because, had the striker scored directly from the rebound, he would have been penalised for touching the ball twice. If you deem the challenge reckless, though, you may caution the defender for unsporting behaviour. **3) Stop play. Make the substitution take place again correctly at the halfway line. The player enters the field of play and the game is restarted with a throw-in.**

2 In added time in a goalless cup tie the away team score. The desperate home captain restarts by shooting straight from the kick-off. The keeper is caught out, and the ball hits the back of the net. What is your decision?

3 The home club, who need a goalless draw for survival, have no ballboys, so every time the ball goes out play is delayed. But with 15 minutes to go, they concede a goal and suddenly ballboys appear. What action, if any, do you take?

1 A long-throw specialist hurls the ball into the goalmouth. Incredibly, it evades everyone, takes a wicked bounce and loops over the keeper into the net. The crowd go wild. Do you give the goal?

2 It has been raining heavily throughout the first half. With water forming on the surface the players have been slipping and sliding about. At half time you are happy that the pitch is still playable, but both teams come to you to insist the game is abandoned. What do you do?

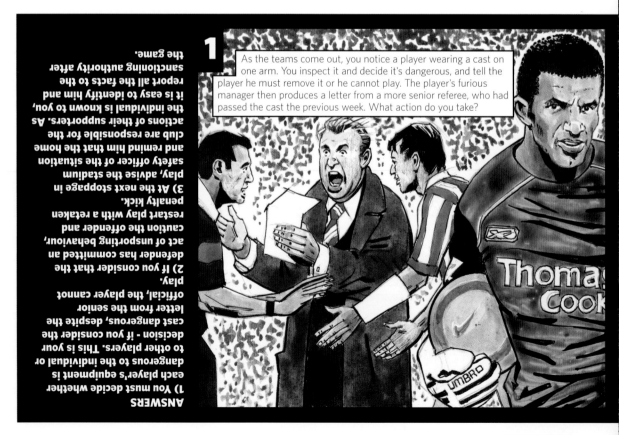

1 As the teams come out, you notice a player wearing a cast on one arm. You inspect it and decide it's dangerous, and tell the player he must remove it or he cannot play. The player's furious manager then produces a letter from a more senior referee, who had passed the cast the previous week. What action do you take?

ANSWERS 1) You must decide whether each player's equipment is dangerous to the individual or to other players. This is your decision - if you consider the cast dangerous, despite the letter from the senior official, the player cannot play. **2)** If you consider that the defender has committed an act of unsporting behaviour, caution the offender and restart play with a retaken penalty kick. **3)** At the next stoppage in play, advise the stadium safety officer of the situation and remind him that the home club are responsible for the actions of their supporters. As the individual is known to you, it is easy to identify him and report all the facts to the sanctioning authority after the game.

3

A defender misjudges the flight of a cross into the penalty area and deliberately tries to swat the ball to safety with his hand. But he misses. What action do you take, if any?

ANSWERS

1) A goal cannot be scored directly from a throw. Restart play with a goal-kick.

2) Abandon the game, taking into account the fact that the teams are the ones who are performing in those conditions. In the Premiership, you must notify the club officials, police and chief steward then take the teams out to play for a few minutes to allow the execution of the planning and safe egress of spectators from the ground.

3) You cannot intervene. If no contact is made, play on.

2

You've awarded a penalty. Just as the penalty taker is about to strike the ball, an opponent shouts out a remark about the penalty taker's wife. In his fury, the taker slips and miskicks the ball wide. What action do you take?

3

The goalkeeper of the away club used to play for the home team. During the game, you notice the barracking of the keeper from the fans behind the net, including slanderous comments, is being orchestrated by the well known chairman of the home team. What action do you take?

1 During the course of the game you notice that a striker isn't wearing shin guards. What course of action do you take?

2 You blow for full time at the end of a tempestuous match – but as the players are leaving the field, you notice a defender making an obscene gesture to the home spectators. What do you do?

1 You blow for offside. A striker, furious with your decision, blasts the ball into touch, striking a ballboy in the face. The ballboy bursts into tears. What is your decision?

ANSWERS

1) Caution the player for delaying the restart, and restart play with the original offside offence. You have no influence over what the player might wish to do by way of an apology to the ballboy.

2) If you consider his actions an act of dissent against you, caution him. If not, acknowledge what he is doing and remind him it is up to you to decide whether the winger is committing an act of simulation.

3a) There is no action you can take against the goalkeeper. **b)** The crossbar must be repaired or replaced: the use of rope is not permitted. If a repair can be carried out, restart play with a drop ball. If not, abandon the game.

TREVILLION

3 A goalmouth melee takes place. The ball drops to a defender, who, in a panic, decides to get it back to his goalkeeper. To avoid his keeper being penalised for picking the ball up, the defender drops down and uses his knee to pass the ball back. What action do you take, if any?

ANSWERS
1) Stop play and tell the player to leave the field to correct his equipment: good-quality shin guards must be covered entirely by the stockings. He may only return during a stoppage in play, after you have checked his guards.
2) Show the player the red card for offensive or insulting or abusive language and/or gestures. You can take this action from the moment you enter the field of play until the moment you leave it after the final whistle.
3) In normal play, a player may use his head, chest or knee to pass back a bouncing ball without being penalised. However, if you feel certain that a player has consciously used his knee as a deliberate attempt to circumvent the backpass law, you must award an indirect free-kick from the place where the infringement occurred.

2 A defender is clearly frustrated with a diving winger and makes his point by coming up to you, pointing at the winger then throwing himself to the ground theatrically. Everyone laughs. How do you react?

3 With play at the other end, a goalkeeper decides on some stretching exercises using the crossbar, which breaks under his weight. a) What action do you take, if any, against the goalkeeper? b) The groundsman suggests stringing a tight rope between the posts. Is this temporary crossbar sufficient?

1 In the tunnel before the match, a fuming player viciously headbutts an opponent. You show the aggressor the red card for violent conduct. His manager then asks if he can replace the red-carded player with another player from his squad, and start with a team of 11. What is your decision?

2 In extremely windy weather, a goalkeeper with a renowned long throw hurls the ball upfield. It is caught by a freak gust of wind, and bounces over the stunned opposition keeper into the back of the net. Do you give the goal?

1 You are the fourth official. During the first 10 minutes of the match, the referee collapses with a torn hamstring and you replace him. Five minutes later, in a goalmouth melee, you are knocked to the ground, breaking your wrist. You can't go on – and only two fit officials remain. What action do you take?

ANSWERS
1) An announcement is made in an effort to find a suitably qualified official among the crowd who can run the line. If no one suitable is available the match may have to be abandoned and the facts reported to the relevant authorities. (Some competitions permit the game to be completed with two officials where there can be no agreement on a suitable replacement.)
2) You ask the player to leave the field of play, the goal stands and you report all the facts to the competition and sanctioning authority at the end of the game. You will almost certainly face a suspension.
3) You advise the player he will only be allowed to play if the offending remarks are removed or covered up. You must inspect the cast once this is done to ensure the remarks are no longer visible. You must also report the matter to the authorities.

3 Midway through a tempestuous relegation clash, serious violence erupts with all 22 players exchanging fierce punches. It is completely out of control. What do you do?

ANSWERS
**1) A player who has been sent off before the kick-off may be replaced – but only by one of the named substitutes.
2) Award a goal, provided that no infringement of the Laws has been committed by the team scoring the goal before the ball enters the net.
3) You must observe until the confrontation subsides, then talk to both assistants to assess the extent of the incident. You may decide to either a) impose appropriate disciplinary sanctions against individuals and restart the game or b) abandon the game, and report the full facts to the authorities.**

2 Near the end of a frantic cup tie, you send off a home player. Amid uproar, the player's manager quickly brings on a sub. In your distracted state, you fail to notice that the man being replaced is the player you've just sent off. Three minutes later the sub scores a dramatic winner. It is only then that you – and the TV cameras – spot your humiliating mistake. What action do you take?

3 As the teams come out at the start of a game, you notice a player is wearing a cast on one arm. You inspect it and decide it is not dangerous, but written on it in large, plainly visible letters is an offensive remark about an opposition player. What action do you take?

1 During a penalty shootout, all 10 players on one side have taken kicks. The eleventh player, who has been suffering from cramp during extra time, pulls up in what appears to be agony as he comes forward to take his kick. He tries to get up, but breaks down each time. However, you know that he missed a penalty in a previous shootout, and suffers from nerves. What action do you take?

2 Early in a game played in heavy rain, you book a player. After a series of incidents, your notebook becomes wet and hard to read. With 10 minutes left, you caution the same player. Five minutes later, he scores a goal, you go to write it down then realise the player concerned has played on after receiving two cautions. What do you do?

1 A cup tie goes to penalties. The home captain demands the penalties be taken in front of the home fans, the away captain demands you use the opposite end. How do you decide?

ANSWERS 1) You must decide based on the toss of a coin. However, the end may also be decided before kick-off by the police ground commander for safety reasons. If this is the case, you must tell both clubs before kick-off. **2)** Goals consist of two upright posts and a bar, so this would not be allowed. If no repair is possible, you must abandon the game. **3)** The fact that the player is not 'in play' is irrelevant: show him the red card.

3

A disaffected maverick player has lost faith in his team and manager. After a series of arguments, he deliberately takes up offside positions, leading you to blow up on every attack his side makes. His team have used all their substitutions, but his apoplectic manager demands the player gets off the pitch. The player refuses. What action do you take?

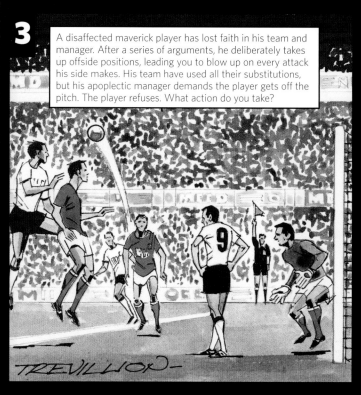

TREVILLION

2

During a Sunday league game at a municipal park, a striker smashes the ball against the home crossbar, which collapses. The away side offer to remove their crossbar to even things up and play on. What do you decide?

3

A player leaves the field for treatment. Before you wave him back on, he re-enters the field and kicks the opponent who injured him. What is your decision?

1 A defender puts in a hard challenge against a nippy winger who screams and rolls around in agony. It helps convince you that the challenge was serious foul play, so you show the defender the red card. But as the defender walks off, you hear the winger laughing. What do you do?

2 In a high-tension play-off final you award a penalty. With stewards slow to respond, a furious fan runs on to the pitch to attack you. Just as he reaches you, a player springs to your aid, punching the spectator and knocking him out. What action do you take, if any?

1 During a relegation battle, the home side concede their fourth goal. As the ball goes in, you see a fracas near the dugouts and notice the home club's manager strike his assistant. What action do you take?

ANSWERS 1) Award the goal, then order the manager to stand away from the technical area and report the matter to the authorities. **2)** Providing the lines are distinctive you must allow the game to go ahead, then report the matter for reference. The Laws only state lines must be distinctive: for instance, in snowy conditions, you may add a red dye to the marking material. **3)** You award an indirect free-kick for offside.

3 A thunderous shot screams towards goal. It beats the keeper, but just before it crosses the line it punctures and loses its shape. Do you award the goal?

ANSWERS
1) You cannot change your decision, but you can make a note of the winger's reaction in your report. If the defender's club believes that your red card was incorrect, they can appeal against your decision.
2) You must show the player the red card.
3) The goal is not awarded. You must restart play with a new ball dropped at the place where the original ball became deflated.

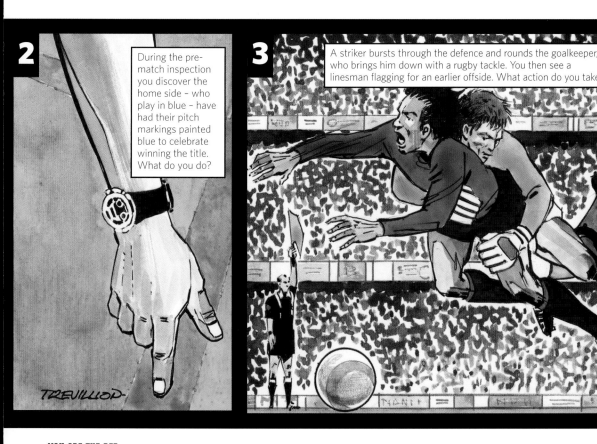

2 During the pre-match inspection you discover the home side – who play in blue – have had their pitch markings painted blue to celebrate winning the title. What do you do?

3 A striker bursts through the defence and rounds the goalkeeper, who brings him down with a rugby tackle. You then see a linesman flagging for an earlier offside. What action do you take?

WORLD CUP SPECIAL

1 A second round tie between France and Spain goes to penalties. Fabien Barthez, in goal for France, comes off his line for the first shot, so you order a retake. He does it again for the second. He's already been booked. What do you do?

2 You are in charge of a group stage game between South Korea and Togo. You award a free-kick against a Korean player, who reacts by snarling at you in a low menacing voice. A team-mate pulls him away. You don't speak Korean and cannot be sure if it is foul and abusive language. What do you decide?

1 A player tries to take a quick throw-in, but an opponent jumps up immediately in front of him. What action do you take, if any?

ANSWERS 1) The law changed at the start of this season and the opponent has to stand no less than two metres from the ball. If the opponent unfairly distracts or impedes the thrower he will be cautioned. **2)** Award the goal and try not to show too much embarrassment. **3)** Show the player the yellow card. Smoking counts as unsporting behaviour – Fifa and Uefa have also issued circulars banning smoking in dugouts and technical areas. In the summer of 2005, Australian referee Mark Shield took action against an Argentine coach under this rule.

3 Ronaldo is heading for an unguarded net against Germany when a streaker who has entered the field rugby tackles him. As the ball bounces away to safety, an enraged Ronaldo stamps on the streaker. What do you do?

ANSWERS
1) You must order another re-take and make it completely clear to him that his actions are not acceptable, and that he risks receiving a yellow card for unsporting behaviour . If he does it again, show him the yellow, then the red. **2)** You must take the player to one side and make it clear through gestures and facial expressions that his behaviour is unacceptable. **3)** Ronaldo must be dismissed for violent conduct.

2 Deep into injury time in a play-off final with the score 1-1, the ball is fired across a crowded penalty area. It evades all outfield players – but it strikes your leg and flies into the net. What do you decide?

3 During a cup final in Tbilisi, a veteran Italian striker goes down injured. You play on as he receives attention on the touchline. The physio hands him a cigarette which he smokes while being treated. What action do you take, if any?

WORLD CUP SPECIAL

1

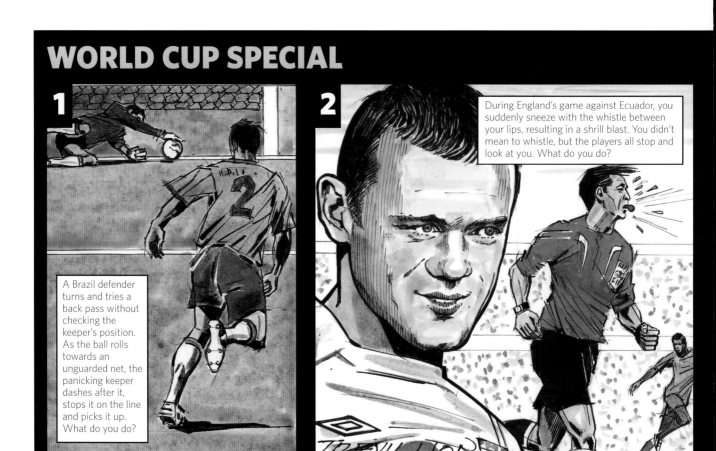

A Brazil defender turns and tries a back pass without checking the keeper's position. As the ball rolls towards an unguarded net, the panicking keeper dashes after it, stops it on the line and picks it up. What do you do?

2

During England's game against Ecuador, you suddenly sneeze with the whistle between your lips, resulting in a shrill blast. You didn't mean to whistle, but the players all stop and look at you. What do you do?

WORLD CUP SPECIAL

1

Portugal's Ronaldo, dribbling at high speed on the touchline, tricks the last man with a step-over. As he races on, a Mexico substitute, warming up at the side of the pitch, sticks a leg out and trips him. What do you do?

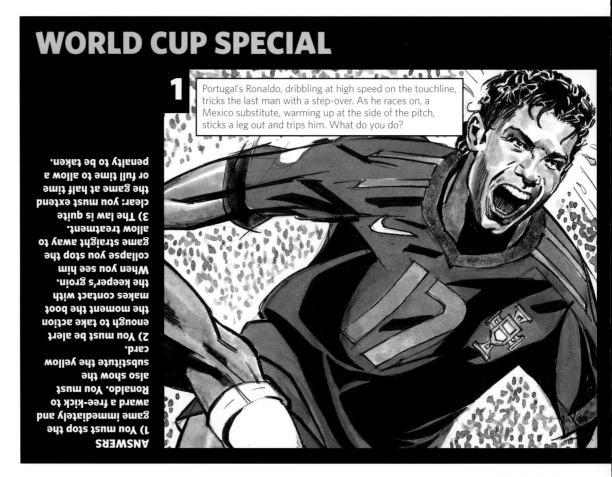

ANSWERS 1) You must stop the game immediately and award a free-kick to Ronaldo. You must also show the substitute the yellow card. **2)** You must be alert enough to take action the moment the boot makes contact with the keeper's groin. When you see him collapse you stop the game straight away to allow treatment. **3)** The law is quite clear: you must extend the game at half time or full time to allow a penalty to be taken.

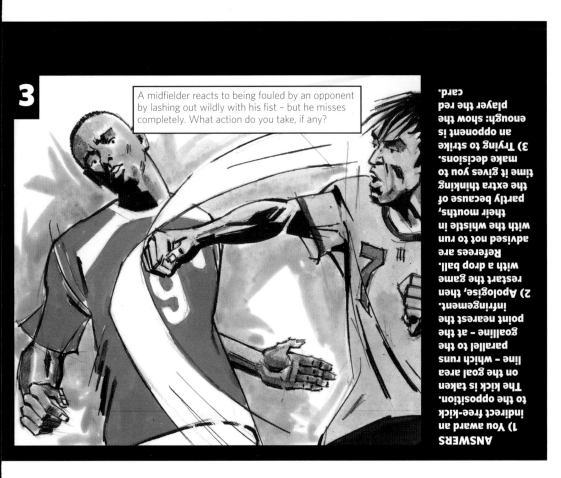

3 A midfielder reacts to being fouled by an opponent by lashing out wildly with his fist – but he misses completely. What action do you take, if any?

2 An Argentina striker races into the area, but as the ball comes to him it bobbles: he air-kicks wildly and his boot flies off and strikes Edwin van der Sar in the groin. As the keeper collapses in agony, the ball runs on to another striker, who scores into an empty net. What do you do?

3 You award a penalty to Spain in the dying seconds of their match against Tunisia. But after all the arguing subsides you notice that, before the kick is taken, your watch shows 90 minutes plus stoppage time has been played. Do you blow for full time?

WORLD CUP SPECIAL

1

A defender walks out before a match holding hands with a mascot. The mascot, in a stroppy mood, sticks out his tongue then kicks the defender. The defender retaliates by cuffing the boy, who cries out in apparent pain. What, if anything, do you do?

TREVILLION

2

In a semi-final, a midfielder commits a vicious lunging challenge from behind. You show him an instant red card – but the defender, in tears, refuses to leave the field. Team-mates try to drag him off, but he falls to his knees, refusing to move. What do you do?

WORLD CUP SPECIAL

1

An attacker commits four offences simultaneously: running offside, handling the ball, deliberately handing off a defender and shouting obscenities at you. What punishment does he earn and how is play restarted?

ANSWERS 1) Send him off. You must punish the most serious of the four offences, which in this case is shouting obscenities. Then you must restart play from the point where the player was offside and deemed active. If a similar situation occurred where all four offences were of a minor nature, you would have to give the offside decision precedence. **2)** You don't have time for a debate: show him the red card for using an insulting gesture. **3)** Award a corner kick. The assistant, like you as referee, is considered part of the field of play.

3

In the 85th minute of a semi-final a team struggling to hold on to a lead make a substitution. The player being subbed – already on a yellow card – strolls off the pitch deliberately slowly. With him now off the field, you show him a second yellow, then a red, for time-wasting. Can the sub still come on, and the team continue with 11 men?

ANSWERS
1) You must show the defender the red card for violent conduct. The matter would be dealt with by the authorities and then passed on to the Child Protection Agency.
2) Play cannot be restarted until the sent-off player leaves the field of play. If his team-mates can't convince him, you must involve security. The player would subsequently receive further sanction.
3) You have dismissed the player: the sub can't come on.

2

Before the final an Italian player performs a Nazi salute during the National Anthem. You challenge him, and he explains that it is traditionally a Roman salute from the time of the Empire. What do you do?

3

A defender under pressure attempts to kick the ball into touch for a throw-in but the ball strikes an over-eager linesman who has encroached slightly on to the pitch. The ball is deflected over the goalline. Is play restarted with a throw-in, corner or goal-kick?

TREVILLION

1

A player with a reputation for diving goes to ground for the fifth time in the match after what appears to be an innocuous challenge. You let play go on as he lies on the pitch motionless. His team-mates begin to get agitated, but their opponents, on the attack, refuse to kick the ball out. Do you intervene?

2

A last-minute shot is deflected by a defender and sails over the middle of the crossbar. The attacking team want to take the corner from the right, the defending team, knowing the opposition have a right-footed corner specialist, demand it be taken from the left. What is your decision?

TREDILLION

1

You award a drop ball in the penalty area. The captain of the home side tells you he wants his keeper to take part – and insists the keeper can use his hands. What is your response?

ANSWERS

1) Allow the keeper to take part – there's nothing in the laws of the game which prevents him. However, the ball is only deemed in play when it touches the ground, so the keeper can only touch it once it has dropped. If he touches it before that point, the drop-ball is retaken. Keith Hackett: 'When I was officiating I'd always try to avoid having a drop-ball in the area. On the odd occasion it happened, I told both players that, in the spirit of the game, the defending side should be allowed to gain possession. It was always accepted by both players.'

2) Award a free-kick to the opposition. Keith Hackett: 'Handling outside the area does cause a lot of debate. People often think a goalkeeper handling outside the box is an automatic red: that's not true – it's only a red card if the keeper has denied an opponent an obvious scoring opportunity.'

3) Restart play with a goal-kick to the defending team.

3 You're in charge of your first Premiership match and your nerves are on edge. Seeing a reckless challenge, you dash over and whip out your yellow card – but to your horror, you suddenly realise you're brandishing the red by mistake. The player is already storming off the field. Can you reverse your 'decision'?

ANSWERS

1) You have a duty of care towards the players of both teams: regardless of reputations, you must err on the side of safety and stop play. Keith Hackett: Some years ago I was officiating Manchester United v Wimbledon when Bryan Robson attempted a diving header. He was knocked unconscious and swallowed his tongue. I stopped play immediately; the quick reaction from United's physio meant Bryan's airway was cleared, and he was taken to hospital.

2) You are paid to make these decisions, and make them clearly and quickly. Before any dispute has a chance to arise, signal clearly with your arm, pointing towards the corner from which you intend the kick to be taken. Hold this pose to ensure every player can see it.

3) You have to admit your error quickly and apologise to the player, bringing him back on to the field of play. At the end of the game, you must then report yourself to the Football Association, who will deal with you as they see fit.

2 A goalkeeper rushes to the edge of his area and safely collects the ball. However, an inrushing defender, trying to help, accidentally collides with the keeper, knocking him – still holding the ball – outside the area. What do you do?

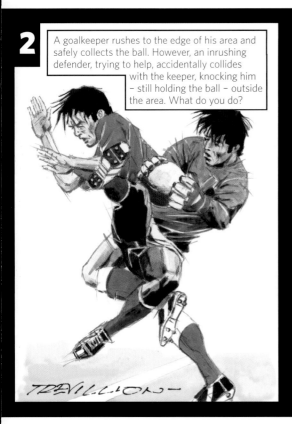

3 A midfield free-kick specialist is lining up an indirect free-kick, as clearly signalled by you. However, he whips the ball in at such speed that it goes straight into the net past the stranded keeper, without being touched by anyone else. How do you restart play?

1

You award a throw-in to the defending side, overruling your assistant. The defender takes a quick throw – but then you notice his team-mate grinning and pointing at you. You realise you've made a mistake. Can you stop play and reverse your decision?

ANSWER No. You'll have to keep the game going, but an apologetic look towards your assistant will help. Keith Hackett: I've kitted Premiership officials out with a communication system so they can talk to each other, so this type of error should be avoided.

2

During a League Two game, a heavy challenge clatters the corner flag and it snaps in half. You stop the game and call for a replacement – but a sheepish stadium manager informs you there is no spare flag. What do you do?

ANSWER Abandon the game and put in a report to the authorities. Keith Hackett: I'd be shocked if a club didn't have replacement flags – they're essential. I remember Jack Taylor delaying the start of the 1974 World Cup final until the corner flags had been put in. He then awarded a penalty in the first minute. He was a great referee and this year celebrates his 50th year in football: what an achievement. When the gongs are next handed out, they should think of him.

3

During a high-tempo game you hear a veteran defender call the opposition winger, who comes from Japan, a 'cheating Chinaman'. Do you take any action?

ANSWER Red card. Keith Hackett: This type of comment is unacceptable: it's racist. Players and fans have been reminded they cannot shout racist remarks at opponents or officials.

INDEX

Teams referred to are those the players represented at the time of drawing.

STANLEY MATTHEWS
(Blackpool)

DANNY BLANCHFLOWER
(Tottenham)